# ABOUT THE AUTHOR

Hello! My name is Igor Doin, and I am a passionate and dedicated professional in the area of information security. With years of practical experience, I have had the privilege of working closely with over 500 companies, helping them strengthen their defenses and ensure the integrity of their systems and data. My cybersecurity journey began with a deep curiosity and enthusiasm for the field, and evolved into a strategic consulting role where I can make a real difference to the security of my clients.

As an ethical hacker, I find great satisfaction in identifying and reporting vulnerabilities in websites and applications. This work is not just a profession for me, but a true passion. The practical experience I have accumulated over the years allows me to understand threats and challenges from different perspectives, which is key to providing effective and personalized solutions.

I currently manage strategic and commercial processes at an information security consultancy company. In this role, I closely monitor each client's journey, from the first contact and assessment of the current situation to continuous improvements over the months. My mission is to ensure that every organization not only achieves, but maintains a robust level of security.

Throughout my career, I have met thousands of people across Brazil and witnessed first-hand the transformation of information security from an often underestimated concept to the solid and essential foundation of any company. Information security is more than a pillar; It is the foundation on which an organization's trust and resilience is built.

I hope this book provides you with valuable and practical insights to improve the security of your own organization. I look forward to sharing with you the lessons learned and best practices I've developed along my cybersecurity journey.

If you like the book, don't forget to leave your review on Amazon, it helps and motivates me a lot! Also, feel free to reach out to me on social media, like Linkedin or Instagram, to tell me how this book helped your career. Now yes: I wish you an excellent read!

# INTRODUCTION

## The Mission of the Cybersecurity Manager

The role of the cybersecurity manager is fundamental to the health and integrity of an organization. An information security manager is someone who occupies a strategic position and is responsible for defining, implementing and supervising a company's security policies and strategies. This role may include positions such as Chief Information Security Officer (CISO), Director of Information Security, or Information Security Manager, among others. The manager's mission is to ensure that the organization is protected against cyber threats and that its security posture is robust and effective.

### The Role of the Manager

The cybersecurity manager is responsible for several crucial tasks:

1. **Development of Security Strategies**: Creates and implements policies and practices that aim to protect the company's assets against threats and vulnerabilities.
2. **Risk Management**: Continuously assesses security risks and implements measures to mitigate those risks. This involves carrying out risk assessments, developing business continuity plans and responding to incidents.
3. **Resource Allocation**: Decides on the resources needed for information security, including budget, tools and personnel.
4. **Compliance and Regulation**: Ensures that the

organization complies with data protection and information security laws and regulations.

5. **Education and Awareness**: Develops training and awareness programs to ensure all employees understand and follow security policies.

## The Importance of the Manager

The importance of the cybersecurity manager to the life of a company cannot be underestimated. They are the guardians of sensitive information and play a crucial role in protecting against cyberattacks that can cause significant financial and reputational damage. In a scenario where cyber threats are becoming increasingly sophisticated, the manager's ability to anticipate, identify and mitigate these risks is vital for the organization's continuity and success.

## Challenges Faced

Cybersecurity managers face a series of complex challenges:

1. **Continuous Evolution of Threats**: Cyber threats are constantly evolving, and the manager must always be up to date with the latest trends and attack techniques to protect the company adequately.

2. **Balance between Security and Usability**: You must strike a balance between implementing rigorous security measures and maintaining the efficiency and functionality of the company's systems and operations.

3. **Limited Resource Management**: Managers often have to deal with restricted budgets and must prioritize investments in security in order to obtain the greatest possible return.

4. **Regulatory Compliance**: Maintaining compliance with a variety of regulations and standards can be challenging, especially when dealing with different jurisdictions and industries.

5. **Organizational Culture**: Promoting a culture of security

within the organization and ensuring that all employees understand and respect security policies can be a significant challenge.

**Final Considerations**

The mission of the cybersecurity manager is, therefore, a complex and multifaceted task. It requires a combination of technical knowledge, management skills and a strategic vision to protect the organization against threats and ensure business continuity. By assuming this role, the manager not only protects the integrity of the company's systems and data, but also contributes to building a robust security culture that strengthens organizational resilience.

The role of a manager is vitally important, and success in this role can have a profound and positive impact on the overall health and safety of an organization. In an ever-changing cyber environment, the manager's skill and dedication are essential to ensure that the company can face future challenges with confidence and security.

**Importance of Information Security for C-Level**

Information security has become a strategic priority for organizations, especially at the C-Level level. With the increasing sophistication of cyber threats and the dependence of business operations on technology, senior executives need to be deeply involved in protecting the company's information assets. Failure to pay adequate attention to security can result in significant financial losses, reputational damage and loss of customer trust.

# Objectives of the Book

This book aims to provide an in-depth, detailed analysis of information security from the perspective of senior executives. Our intention is to enable leaders and managers to fully understand the complexities and nuances of cybersecurity, providing them with the tools and knowledge necessary to make well-informed strategic decisions.

Through this book, we aim to:

1. **Develop a Comprehensive View of Information Security**: Provide a holistic understanding of information security concepts and practices, highlighting their importance for the protection and integrity of corporate operations.
2. **Empower Executives to Make Informed Decisions**: Equip leaders with the essential knowledge to assess risks, implement effective security measures, and make strategic choices that promote organizational resilience.
3. **Guide the Implementation of Effective Security Strategies**: Provide practical guidance and proven strategies for developing and executing security policies and procedures that meet the specific needs of your organizations.
4. **Promote the Creation of a Resilient Corporate Culture**: Encourage the construction of an organizational culture that values and integrates information security at all levels, ensuring that all employees are aligned with the best security practices and prepared to face cyber threats.
5. **Prepare for the Future of Information Security**: Discuss emerging trends and technological innovations in the area of cybersecurity, helping executives prepare for future challenges and adopt innovative solutions that strengthen their organizations' security posture.

Throughout the book, we seek not only to clarify the technical and strategic aspects of information security, but also to inspire and empower leaders to become proactive defenders of cybersecurity in their companies. With a focus on effective practices and creating a robust security culture, this book serves as an essential guide for any executive committed to protecting and strengthening their organization against cyber threats.

## Chapter Overview

1. Understanding Information Security: Definition, scope, threats, vulnerabilities and impacts on companies.
2. The Role of the C-Level in Information Security: Responsibilities, involvement, security culture and leadership examples.
3. Policies and Governance: Development of policies, governance frameworks, compliance and regulations.
4. Risk Management: Assessment, risk mitigation, business continuity and case studies.
5. Security Implementation Strategies: Essential technologies, integration of security into business processes and cloud security.
6. Security and Innovation: Impact of digital transformation, security in IoT, AI, Blockchain and protection of innovations.
7. Communication and Training: Employee involvement, training programs and effective communication.
8. Incident Response and Crisis Management: Response plans, incident response teams and crisis communication.
9. Measuring Success: KPIs, reports, security audits and continuous improvements.
10. The Future of Information Security: Trends, new threats, innovations and opportunities.

# CHAPTER 1: UNDERSTANDING INFORMATION SECURITY

## Definition and Scope

Information security is the set of practices, policies and strategies developed to protect an organization's data and information against unauthorized access, misuse, disclosure, interruption, modification or destruction. The scope of information security is vast, encompassing not only digital data stored on computers, servers and mobile devices, but also physical information such as printed documents and paper records.

Information security is based on three fundamental pillars, known as the CIA model:

1. **Confidentiality:** Ensures that information is only accessible by authorized people. This implies access restrictions, data encryption and strict access control practices.
2. **Integrity:** Ensures that data is accurate and complete, protected from unauthorized changes. This involves implementing mechanisms to detect and prevent malicious or accidental changes to data.

3. **Availability:** Ensures information and resources are available to authorized users when needed. This includes implementing redundancies, backups, and disaster recovery plans to minimize downtime.

Information security is essential for all organizations, regardless of size or sector, as it protects valuable assets and ensures business continuity.

# Main Threats and Vulnerabilities

To develop effective defenses, it is crucial to understand the main threats and vulnerabilities that can affect information security. Threats can be categorized as internal or external:

1. **Insider Threats:** They include malicious or negligent actions by employees, former employees, contractors or business partners. Common examples are:
   o **Insider Threats:** Employees who abuse authorized access to steal or damage data.
   o **Human Error:** Inadvertent failures, such as disclosing sensitive information by mistake or improperly configuring systems.
2. **External Threats:** They originate outside the organization and include cyber attacks, espionage and fraud. Examples include:
   o **Malware:** Malicious software, such as viruses, worms, Trojans, and spyware, designed to cause damage or steal information.
   o **Ransomware:** Type of malware that encrypts the victim's data and demands payment of a ransom to restore access.
   o **Phishing:** Social engineering attacks that trick users into revealing sensitive information, such as passwords and credit card numbers.
   o **Denial of Service (DoS) Attacks:** Attacks that aim to

make a service or network unavailable by overloading it with malicious traffic.

○ **Corporate Espionage:** The act of obtaining confidential commercial information through illicit methods.

In addition to threats, it is vital to recognize vulnerabilities that can be exploited by these attacks:

- **Software Vulnerabilities:** Errors or flaws in the code that can be exploited to gain unauthorized access or cause damage.
- **Incorrect Settings:** Poor configuration of systems, networks or applications that leaves security holes.
- **Weak Passwords:** Using easy-to-guess passwords or reusing passwords across multiple services.
- **Lack of Updates:** Outdated systems and software that do not have the latest security patches.
- **Insecure Networks:** Using networks without adequate encryption, such as public Wi-Fi networks.

# Security Impacts on Companies

Security breaches can have devastating consequences for businesses, affecting them in several ways:

1. **Financial Loss:** Direct costs associated with incident response, data recovery, regulatory fines, and ransom payments. Additionally, there are indirect losses such as lost revenue due to business interruption and litigation costs.
2. **Damage to Reputation:** The trust of customers, partners and investors can be severely shaken following a data breach. Companies like Target and Equifax have suffered major damage to their public image following security incidents.
3. **Regulatory Penalties:** Many jurisdictions have strict

data protection laws, such as GDPR in Europe and CCPA in California. Violations of these regulations can result in substantial fines and additional compliance obligations.

4. **Operational Interruptions:** Cyberattacks can cause significant downtime, affecting a company's ability to operate normally. Ransomware, for example, can encrypt critical systems, requiring considerable time and resources to restore operations.

Notable examples of security breaches include:

- **Target (2013):** A malware attack affected approximately 40 million credit and debit cards, resulting in financial losses, reputational damage and compliance costs.
- **Equifax (2017):** A data breach exposed the personal information of approximately 147 million people, leading to significant fines, loss of customer trust, and massive recovery costs.

Understanding and mitigating these threats and vulnerabilities is essential to protect the organization against adverse impacts and ensure business continuity.

# CHAPTER 2: THE MANAGER'S ROLE IN INFORMATION SECURITY

## C-Level Responsibilities and Involvement

C-Level executives play a crucial role in information security. They are responsible for ensuring that security is a strategic priority and that all levels of the organization are aligned with that vision. The responsibilities and involvement of C-Level executives can be described as follows:

1. **Definition of Vision and Strategy:** Executives must establish a clear vision for information security, aligned with the organization's business objectives. This includes setting goals and creating a comprehensive strategy that addresses all aspects of security.

2. **Resource Allocation:** Information security requires significant investments in technology, people and processes. C-Level executives must ensure that adequate resources are allocated to implement and maintain effective security measures.

3. **Creation of Security Policies:** Executives are responsible for approving and promoting robust security policies. These policies must cover all critical areas such as access

management, data protection, incident response and regulatory compliance.

4. **Supervision and Governance:** It is critical that executives continually monitor the state of information security. This involves regularly reviewing security reports, audits and risk assessments to ensure that protective measures are working as expected.

5. **Engagement and Communication:** Executives must actively engage in communicating about the importance of information security. This includes regular meetings with security teams, participation in training and awareness campaigns, and promoting a culture of security throughout the organization.

# Corporate Security Culture

Developing a solid security culture is essential for effectively protecting information assets. This involves:

1. **Exemplary Leadership:** Leaders must demonstrate a genuine commitment to safety by serving as a role model for all employees. When senior management prioritizes security, it positively influences behavior across the organization.

2. **Training and Awareness:** Regular training programs and awareness campaigns are key to educating employees about safe practices. This includes teaching about common threats like phishing and social engineering and how to respond appropriately.

3. **Continuous Communication:** Open and ongoing communication about security issues is crucial. Executives should promote security discussions in meetings, newsletters, and other internal communication channels.

4. **Incentives and Rewards:** Recognizing and rewarding

behaviors that contribute to safety can motivate employees to adopt safe practices. This may include awards for teams or individuals who demonstrate safety excellence.

5. **Integration with Business Processes:** Security must be integrated into daily business processes. This means that all operations, from new product development to customer service, must consider security as a central component.

# Examples of Security Leadership

Case studies of companies that have demonstrated leadership in information security can provide valuable insights:

1. **Microsoft:** Microsoft is recognized for its proactive approach to security. The company has implemented the concept of "Security in Depth", which involves multiple layers of defense to protect against threats. Additionally, Microsoft invests significantly in security research and collaborates with the global community to continually improve its security practices.

2. **IBM:** IBM has a long history of security innovation. The company uses artificial intelligence and machine learning to detect and respond to threats in real time. IBM also promotes a strong security culture by providing ongoing training and encouraging collaboration between its security teams and other business units.

3. **Google:** Google has implemented a "Bug Bounty" program, which rewards security researchers for identifying and reporting vulnerabilities in its systems. This approach not only improves the security of Google products, but also demonstrates the company's commitment to transparency and collaborative security.

These examples illustrate how information security leadership can be achieved through a combination of strategy, investment and organizational culture. C-Level executives must learn from these practices and adapt the lessons to the specific needs and contexts of their own organizations.

# CHAPTER 3: POLICIES AND GOVERNANCE

## Development of Security Policies

Developing well-defined security policies is essential to protecting an organization's information assets. These policies must be clear, comprehensive and aligned with business objectives. Here are the essential steps and considerations for developing effective security policies:

1. **Needs Analysis:** Identify the organization's specific security needs, considering the nature of the data it handles, the risks faced, and applicable regulatory requirements.
2. **Stakeholder Involvement:** Collaborate with multiple stakeholders, including IT, human resources, legal, operations, and senior management, to ensure security policies meet the needs of the entire organization.
3. **Definition of Objectives:** Establish clear objectives for security policies, such as protecting data confidentiality, integrity, and availability, ensuring regulatory compliance, and mitigating risks.
4. **Detailed Documentation:** Develop detailed policies that cover all critical aspects of information security, such as access control, incident management, data protection, physical security, and cybersecurity.
5. **Communication and Implementation:** Communicate

security policies to all employees and stakeholders. Provide training to ensure everyone understands their responsibilities and knows how to follow policies.

6. **Review and Update:** Security policies should be regularly reviewed and updated to reflect changes in legislation, technology and security threats. Establish a formal process for periodically reviewing and updating policies.

# Governance Frameworks (ISO 27001, NIST, etc.)

Governance frameworks provide a systematic framework for managing information security, helping organizations align their security practices with international standards and best practices. Here are two of the most recognized frameworks:

1. **ISO 27001:**
   o **Structure and Benefits:** ISO 27001 is an international standard for information security management systems (ISMS). It provides a process-based approach to establishing, implementing, operating, monitoring, reviewing, maintaining and improving information security.
   o **Implementation:** Implementing ISO 27001 involves carrying out a risk assessment, defining appropriate security controls, documenting an ISMS and continually auditing the system to ensure compliance.
   o **Certification:** ISO 27001 certification can demonstrate to customers and partners that the organization adopts the best information security practices, increasing trust and credibility.
2. **NIST (National Institute of Standards and Technology):**
   o **Structure and Benefits:** The NIST framework provides

detailed guidelines for managing cybersecurity. It is widely used by organizations in the United States and is compliant with several international standards.

- Main Components: The NIST framework is comprised of five main functions: Identify, Protect, Detect, Respond, and Recover. These functions help organizations comprehensively manage and reduce cyber risk.
- Implementation: Implementing the NIST framework involves identifying critical assets, protecting against cyber threats, detecting security incidents, responding to incidents, and recovering after incidents.

# Compliance and Regulations

Compliance with information security regulations is crucial to avoid legal penalties, protect customer data and maintain stakeholder trust. Regulations vary by industry and geographic location, but some of the most important include:

1. **GDPR (General Data Protection Regulation):**
   - **Scope and Requirements:** GDPR is a European Union data protection regulation that applies to all organizations that process personal data of EU residents. Requirements include obtaining explicit consent for data processing, guaranteeing individuals' right to privacy, and notifying data breaches within 72 hours.
   - **Penalties:** GDPR violations can result in significant fines, up to 4% of the organization's global annual revenue or €20 million, whichever is greater.
2. **HIPAA (Health Insurance Portability and Accountability Act):**
   - **Scope and Requirements:** HIPAA is a United States regulation that establishes standards for the protection

of protected health information (PHI). Requirements include implementing administrative, physical, and technical safeguards to ensure the confidentiality, integrity, and availability of PHI.

- **Penalties:** Violations of HIPAA can result in civil and criminal fines depending on the severity and nature of the violation.

3. **PCI-DSS (Payment Card Industry Data Security Standard):**

- **Scope and Requirements:** PCI-DSS is a set of security requirements for all entities that store, process or transmit payment card data. Requirements include implementing access controls, encrypting card data and conducting vulnerability testing.

- **Penalties:** Failure to comply with PCI-DSS can result in fines imposed by payment card companies, increased transaction fees, and in serious cases, the suspension of the ability to process card payments.

C-Level executives must ensure that the organization complies with all relevant regulations. This involves carrying out regular audits, implementing compliance controls and keeping detailed records of all compliance activities.

# CHAPTER 4: RISK MANAGEMENT

## Risk Assessment and Mitigation

Risk management is an essential practice for information security and involves a systematic process of identifying, evaluating and mitigating potential risks that could compromise the integrity, confidentiality and availability of data. Here are the key steps and effective tools for risk assessment and mitigation:

1. **Risk Identification:**
   - **Asset Inventory:** Take a complete inventory of information assets, including hardware, software, data and personnel.
   - **Threat Identification:** Identify potential threats that could affect assets, such as malware, cyberattacks, hardware failures, natural disasters, and human error.
   - **Vulnerability Identification:** Assess vulnerabilities that can be exploited by threats such as software flaws, lack of security policies, poor password management practices, and outdated systems.
2. **Risk Assessment:**
   - **SWOT Analysis:** Use SWOT analysis (Strengths, Weaknesses, Opportunities, Threats) to identify internal strengths and weaknesses, as well as external opportunities and threats.
   - **Impact Assessment:** Conduct impact assessments

to determine the potential consequences of a security incident. Consider factors such as financial loss, reputational damage, interruption of operations and legal penalties.

o **Risk Classification:** Rank risks based on likelihood of occurrence and potential impact. Use a risk matrix to prioritize risks that need to be mitigated urgently.

3. **Risk Mitigation:**

o **Controls Development:** Develop and implement security controls to mitigate identified risks. This may include technical controls such as firewalls and encryption, administrative controls such as policies and procedures, and physical controls such as access security.

o **Action Plans:** Prepare detailed action plans for each identified risk, specifying the measures to be taken, those responsible for implementation and deadlines for execution.

o **Monitoring and Review:** Establish a continuous process of monitoring and reviewing the risks and controls implemented. Conduct regular audits and review mitigation plans as necessary to ensure their effectiveness.

# Business Continuity and Disaster Recovery Plans

Business continuity plans (BCP) and disaster recovery plans (DRP) are essential to ensure that the organization can continue operating during and after a crisis. These plans must be well designed and tested regularly to ensure their effectiveness. Here are the main components and considerations:

1. **Development of Business Continuity Plans (BCP):**

o **Business Impact Analysis (BIA):** Perform a BIA to

identify critical business processes and determine the potential impact of disruptions. This will help prioritize resources and recovery efforts.

○ **Continuity Strategies:** Develop strategies to ensure the continuity of critical processes, such as system redundancies, alternative work locations, and partnerships with external suppliers.

○ **Communication Plan:** Establish a communications plan to keep stakeholders informed during a crisis. This should include emergency contacts, communication channels and procedures for disseminating information.

2. **Development of Disaster Recovery Plans (DRP):**

○ **Resource Inventory:** Take a complete inventory of the resources needed for recovery, including IT systems, critical data, infrastructure, and personnel.

○ **Recovery Procedures:** Develop detailed procedures for system and data recovery, including regular backups, recovery of critical systems, and recovery testing.

○ **Tests and Training:** Conduct regular DRP testing to identify gaps and areas for improvement. Offer ongoing training for the team involved in executing the plans.

3. **Examples of Real Incidents and Effective Responses:**

○ **Ransomware Attack:** A notable example is the 2017 WannaCry ransomware attack, which affected thousands of organizations around the world. Companies that had up-to-date backups and well-established incident response plans were able to quickly recover their systems.

○ **Natural Disaster:** During Hurricane Katrina in 2005, many businesses were severely impacted. However, organizations that had alternative work locations and robust business continuity strategies were able to maintain their operations.

# Risk Management Case Studies

In-depth case studies are a valuable tool for understanding how different companies have approached risk management, the challenges faced and lessons learned. Here are some examples:

1. **Case Study: Technology Company**
   - **Challenge:** A technology company faced an insider threat when a disgruntled employee tried to steal sensitive data.
   - **Approach:** The company has implemented a strict security policy, including continuous monitoring of employee activities and role-based access restrictions.
   - **Result:** The threat was detected and mitigated quickly, preventing data loss and protecting the integrity of the company.

2. **Case Study: Financial Institution**
   - **Challenge:** A financial institution suffered a targeted phishing attack that compromised customer information.
   - **Approach:** The institution performed a detailed risk analysis, implemented a security awareness training program for employees and customers, and enhanced access and authentication controls.
   - **Result:** The institution was able to significantly reduce the rate of successful phishing attacks and improve the security of customer information.

3. **Case Study: Healthcare Company**
   - **Challenge:** A healthcare company needed to ensure compliance with regulations like HIPAA and protect sensitive health information.
   - **Approach:** The company has implemented an ISMS (Information Security Management System) based on ISO 27001, including regular risk assessments, strict access controls and compliance audits.

- ○ **Result:** The company was able to maintain HIPAA compliance, protect sensitive data, and improve patient trust.

# CHAPTER 5: SECURITY IMPLEMENTATION STRATEGIES

## Essential Technologies and Tools

Implementing an effective security strategy requires the use of technologies and tools that offer comprehensive protection against a variety of threats. Here are some of the essential technologies and tools to consider:

1. **Firewalls:**
   - **Definition and Importance:** Firewalls are security devices that monitor and control network traffic based on pre-determined security rules. They act as a barrier between secure internal networks and external networks, such as the internet.
   - **Types of Firewalls:** There are several types of firewalls, including packet filtering firewalls, stateful inspection firewalls, application firewalls (WAF), and next-generation firewalls (NGFW), which offer advanced functionality such as deep packet inspection and intrusion prevention.
2. **Intrusion Detection and Prevention Systems (IDS/IPS):**
   - **IDS (Intrusion Detection Systems):** Intrusion detection systems monitor the network and systems for suspicious activity and possible violations of security

policies. They alert administrators to potential threats.

- ○ **IPS (Intrusion Prevention Systems):** Intrusion prevention systems not only detect threats, but also take actions to prevent attacks from occurring, such as blocking malicious traffic or restarting compromised services.

3. **Encryption:**
- ○ **Importance of Cryptography:** Encryption is critical to protecting the confidentiality and integrity of data in transit and at rest. It ensures that only authorized parties can access and modify data.
- ○ **Types of Encryption:** Encryption can be symmetric (single key) or asymmetric (public key and private key). Protocols such as SSL/TLS for encrypting data in transit and AES for data at rest are widely used.

4. **Security Monitoring and Management Tools:**
- ○ **SIEM (Security Information and Event Management):** SIEM tools collect, analyze, and correlate security event data from multiple sources to identify patterns and detect security incidents.
- ○ **Patch Management Systems:** Tools that ensure all systems and software are up to date with the latest security fixes to minimize vulnerabilities.

# Security Integration into Business Processes

Integrating security into business processes from the beginning is an essential practice to prevent vulnerabilities and ensure that security is not seen as an obstacle to innovation. Here are some approaches to achieving this:

1. **DevSecOps Practices:**
- ○ **Definition and Benefits:** DevSecOps is the integration of security into the software development

lifecycle (SDLC). It ensures that security is considered at every stage of development, from planning to implementation and maintenance.

o **Security Automation:** Utilize automation tools to perform continuous security testing, such as static code analysis (SAST), dynamic code analysis (DAST), and software dependency vulnerability scanning.

2. **Security by Design:**

o **Security by Design Principles:** Design systems with security in mind from the beginning, incorporating principles such as least privilege, defense in depth, and separation of duties.

o **Threat Modeling:** Perform threat modeling during the design phase to identify and mitigate potential risks before the system is implemented.

3. **Education and Training:**

o **Continuous Training:** Provide ongoing training for developers, system administrators, and other stakeholders on security best practices and new threats.

o **Safety Culture:** Promote an organizational culture that prioritizes security in all business activities, encouraging collaboration between development, operations and security teams.

# Cloud Security and Hybrid Environments

With the growing adoption of cloud solutions and hybrid environments, ensuring security in these contexts is critical to protecting data and maintaining compliance with regulations. Here are some important considerations:

1. **Cloud-Specific Security Policies:**

o **Secure Settings:** Ensure that cloud services security configurations are correct, including the use of role-based access controls (RBAC) and identity and access policies (IAM).

o **Cloud Encryption:** Use encryption to protect data stored and in transit in the cloud. Key management tools (KMS) can help you manage encryption keys securely.

2. **Monitoring and Auditing Tools:**

o **Continuous Monitoring:** Implement continuous monitoring solutions to detect suspicious activity and anomalies in cloud environments.

o **Audit and Compliance:** Conduct regular audits to ensure security policies and compliance practices are being followed. Utilize cloud-specific compliance tools to help maintain compliance with regulations such as GDPR, HIPAA, and PCI-DSS.

3. **Identity and Access Management (IAM):**

o **IAM in the Cloud:** Implement IAM solutions that enable granular control of access to cloud resources. This includes defining access policies based on principles of least privilege and multi-factor authentication (MFA).

o **Security in Hybrid Environments:** Ensure that IAM policies are consistent across hybrid environments, where on-premises and cloud resources are used together.

# CHAPTER 6: SECURITY AND INNOVATION

## Impact of Digital Transformation

Digital transformation is revolutionizing the way companies operate, offering new opportunities to improve efficiency, customer experience and competitiveness. However, this transformation also introduces new challenges for information security. Emerging technologies such as the Internet of Things (IoT), Artificial Intelligence (AI) and Blockchain are changing the cybersecurity landscape, requiring innovative approaches to ensure data protection.

- **Internet of Things (IoT):** With billions of connected devices, IoT significantly expands the attack surface, creating countless opportunities for attackers to exploit vulnerabilities. IoT devices often have inadequate security, which can lead to large-scale security compromises.
- **Artificial Intelligence (AI):** AI offers powerful tools for detecting and responding to cyber threats, but it can also be used by attackers to create more sophisticated attacks. AI needs to be protected against manipulation and adversarial attacks.
- **Blockchain:** Blockchain promises greater security and transparency in transactions, but also faces challenges such as vulnerabilities in smart contracts and 51% attacks. Ensuring security in blockchain-based systems is crucial to

maintaining trust and data integrity.

# Security in IoT, AI and Blockchain

Each of these emerging technologies presents unique risks that require specific security measures. Below, we explore best practices for protecting each of these innovations.

**Internet of Things (IoT):**

- **Best Practices:** Implement robust authentication and identity management for IoT devices. Use encryption to protect data in transit and at rest. Perform regular firmware updates and continuously monitor devices to detect anomalous behavior.
- **Case Study:** A manufacturing company implemented an IoT sensor network to monitor the efficiency of its operations. By adopting a security-by-design approach, including network segmentation and data encryption, they were able to significantly reduce the risk of cyberattacks.

**Artificial Intelligence (AI):**

- **Best Practices:** Integrate security into the AI development lifecycle, ensuring models are trained and tested to withstand adversarial attacks. Protect data used to train AI models to prevent the introduction of malicious data. Continuously monitor AI systems to detect and respond to anomalous behavior.
- **Case Study:** A cybersecurity company has developed an AI-based intrusion detection system. To protect the system, they implemented measures such as integrity checking training data and using explainable machine learning techniques to identify and fix vulnerabilities.

**Blockchain:**

- **Best Practices:** Implement regular smart contract audits to identify and fix vulnerabilities. Use advanced encryption techniques to protect transactions and data stored on the blockchain. Establish clear policies for managing cryptographic keys.

- **Case Study:** An e-commerce platform has adopted blockchain to manage financial transactions. They have implemented regular smart contract audits and utilized robust consensus algorithms to ensure the integrity and security of transactions.

# Protect Technological Innovations

Ensuring that innovation does not compromise security is a delicate balance. Clear security policies and practices integrated into the development process can help protect technological innovations without inhibiting progress. Here are some strategies for achieving that balance:

- **Security by Design:** Taking a security by design approach ensures that security is considered at every stage of new product and technology development. This includes performing risk assessments, threat modeling, and ongoing security testing.
- **Safety Culture:** Fostering an organizational culture that prioritizes security is critical to ensuring that all employees, from developers to executives, understand the importance of security and follow best practices.
- **Continuing Education and Training:** Providing ongoing education and training programs for all employees helps keep staff up to date on the latest security threats and practices. This includes specific training for developers on how to integrate security into software development.
- **Collaboration and Information Sharing:** Collaborating with other organizations and participating in threat intelligence sharing initiatives can help improve your security posture.

This allows companies to learn from each other's experiences and adopt proven practices.

# CHAPTER 7: COMMUNICATION AND TRAINING

## Employee Involvement

Employees are often considered the weakest link in the information security chain, but with the right training, they can become the most effective first line of defense. Employee involvement in information security begins with creating an organizational culture that values and prioritizes security.

**Practical Tips:**

- **Continuing Education:** Offer regular cybersecurity training, updating employees on the latest threats and best practices. Use e-learning modules, workshops and practical simulations to make learning more interactive and effective.
- **Incident Reporting Encouragement:** Establish clear, secure channels so employees can report suspicious activity or potential security breaches without fear of reprisal. Reward employees who proactively identify and report threats.
- **Company-Wide Engagement:** Involve all departments and hierarchical levels in information security. Hold regular meetings to discuss safety issues and encourage active participation from all employees.

**Training and Awareness Programs**

Training and awareness programs are essential to empower employees to recognize and appropriately respond to cyber threats. An effective program must be ongoing and adaptable to changes in the threat landscape.

**Practical Tips:**

- **Diversification of Training Methods:** Utilize a variety of training methods, including videos, quizzes, phishing simulations, and in-person sessions, to keep content interesting and accessible to all employees.
- **Relevant and Updated Content:** Ensure training material is relevant to employees' specific roles and is always up to date with the latest trends and threats. Incorporate real-world case studies to illustrate the importance of security practices.
- **Measurement and Continuous Improvement:** Evaluate the effectiveness of training programs through testing and participant feedback. Use this information to continually improve training content and delivery.

## Effective Safety Communication

Clear and effective communication about security is essential to ensure that everyone in the organization understands the importance of information security and knows how to contribute to protecting the company's assets.

**Practical Tips:**

- **Transparency and Clarity:** Communicate security policies transparently and clearly, avoiding technical jargon whenever possible. Use practical examples to illustrate complex concepts and ensure all employees understand expectations.
- **Diversified Communication Channels:** Utilize different communication channels such as emails, intranet, newsletters, team meetings and corporate communication

applications to reach all employees effectively.

- **Awareness Campaigns:** Conduct regular awareness campaigns, such as "Information Security Week," to keep security top of mind and reinforce the ongoing importance of secure practices. Include expert talks, interactive workshops, and safety challenges with prizes to encourage participation.

**Example of a Successful Communication Strategy:**

- **XYZ Company Case:** Company XYZ implemented a quarterly security awareness campaign that included newsletters, educational videos, and phishing simulations. They also instituted a "Safety Ambassadors" program where employees from different departments were trained to act as safety resources and help disseminate safe information and practices. As a result, the company has seen a significant reduction in security incidents and an increase in early detection of threats by employees.

# CHAPTER 8: INCIDENT RESPONSE AND CRISIS MANAGEMENT

## Incident Response Plans

An incident response plan is essential to minimize the impacts of a security incident and ensure a quick and effective recovery. This plan must be detailed, well structured and adapted to the specific needs of the organization.

**Practical Tips:**

- **Definition of Procedures:** Develop clear procedures to identify, contain, eradicate and recover from security incidents. Include specific steps for different types of incidents, such as data breaches, malware attacks, and account compromises.
- **Designation of Responsibilities:** Specify each team member's responsibilities during an incident. Define who will be responsible for internal and external communication, who will coordinate the technical response, and who will handle legal and compliance aspects.
- **Training and Testing:** Conduct regular training and mock drills to ensure everyone knows how to react during a real incident. Test the plan periodically to identify and correct flaws.

## Incident Response Teams (CSIRT)

Specialized incident response teams, known as Computer Security Incident Response Teams (CSIRT), are fundamental to the effective management of security crises. These teams are made up of qualified professionals who are responsible for coordinating and executing incident response activities.

### Practical Tips:

- **Team Structure:** Define a clear structure for the CSIRT, including permanent members and external consultants if necessary. The team should include security experts, data analysts, communications experts, and legal representatives.
- **Roles and Responsibilities:** Assign specific roles within the CSIRT, such as team leader, response coordinator, incident analyst, and communications officer. Each member must have a clear understanding of their responsibilities and the hierarchy of command during an incident.
- **Coordination and Collaboration:** Establish coordination and collaboration protocols within the CSIRT and with other stakeholders such as security service providers and regulatory authorities. Use secure and effective communication tools to ensure real-time information exchange.

## Communication in Crisis Situations

Effective communication during a security crisis is crucial to controlling the situation, maintaining stakeholder trust and minimizing damage to the organization's reputation. A well-planned and executed approach can make the difference between a smooth recovery and a public relations disaster.

### Practical Tips:

- **Crisis Communication Plan:** Develop a crisis communications plan that includes key messages, communication channels, and designated responsibilities.

Define how and when information will be disclosed internally and externally.

- **Transparency and Trust:** Maintain transparency when reporting security incidents. Provide accurate information and regular updates to stakeholders, preventing the spread of rumors and misinformation.
- **Examples of Good Practices:** Study examples of companies that have managed security crises effectively. Target, for example, took a proactive approach following its data breach, quickly communicating with customers and implementing corrective measures, which helped restore consumer trust.

**Example of Crisis Management:**

- **Equifax case:** Equifax suffered one of the largest data breaches in history, affecting an estimated 147 million people. The company was criticized for its slow and confusing initial response. A detailed study of this case can provide valuable lessons on the importance of a rapid, coordinated and transparent response to security crises.

**Conclusion**

Managing security incidents and crises requires careful planning, specialized teams and effective communication. Implementing a well-structured incident response plan, forming and training a competent CSIRT, and adopting transparent communication practices can significantly reduce negative impacts and facilitate the organization's recovery after an incident.

# CHAPTER 9:
# MEASURING SUCCESS

## Performance Indicators (KPIs)

Measuring the success of information security initiatives is crucial to understanding the impact of implemented strategies and identifying areas in need of improvement. Performance Indicators (KPIs) specific to information security provide objective metrics that help evaluate the effectiveness of security measures.

**Practical Tips:**

- **Definition of Relevant KPIs:** Identify KPIs that align with the organization's security and business objectives. Examples include:
    - **Number of Security Incidents:** Number of incidents detected in a given period.
    - **Incident Response Time:** Average time to detect, contain and resolve a security incident.
    - **False Positive/Negative Rate:** Proportion of security alerts that were incorrectly identified.
    - **Compliance with Security Policies:** Percentage of adherence to internal security policies and procedures.
    - **Effectiveness of Safety Training:** Assessment of improvement in employee awareness after training sessions.
- **Data Collection and Analysis:** Utilize monitoring

and analytics tools to collect accurate, real-time data on KPIs. Tools like SIEM (Security Information and Event Management) can help consolidate and analyze data from multiple sources.

- **Benchmarking:** Compare KPIs to industry benchmarks to assess the organization's relative performance. This can help identify areas where the organization is below average and needs improvement.

## Security Reports and Audits

Regular reporting and security audits are essential components for maintaining transparency, ensuring compliance, and providing insights into the effectiveness of security strategies.

## Practical Tips:

- **Security Reports:** Develop detailed security reports that include incident analysis, compliance status, internal and external audit results, and threat trends. Ensure reports are understandable to different stakeholders, including C-Level executives and IT technicians.
- **Reporting Frequency:** Establish a regular frequency for generating security reports, such as monthly, quarterly, and annual. Frequent reports help keep senior management informed and allow for quick adjustments to security strategies.
- **Security Audits:** Conduct periodic security audits to assess compliance with policies, procedures and regulations. Internal and external audits are important to identify failures and risk areas.
  - **Internal Audits:** Conducted by internal security or audit teams, these assessments help identify and fix issues before they can be exploited.
  - **External Audits:** Audits carried out by independent third parties can provide an unbiased view and identify areas that may have been overlooked by internal teams.

## Continuous Improvements

Information security is a dynamic process that requires continuous adjustments and improvements to remain effective in the face of new threats and emerging technologies.

## Practical Tips:

- **Feedback Structures:** Establish continuous feedback mechanisms to collect information from employees, stakeholders and external experts. Use this information to identify new threats and opportunities for improvement.
- **Regular Reviews:** Conduct regular reviews of security policies, procedures and controls to ensure they are up to date and effective. Consider changes in the threat environment, new technologies, and changes in organizational structure.
- **Continuous Improvement Programs:** Implement continuous improvement programs that encourage innovation and adaptation. Use methodologies such as PDCA (Plan-Do-Check-Act) to guide the continuous improvement process.

## Conclusion

Measuring the success of information security initiatives through KPIs, reports and audits is fundamental to maintaining the effectiveness of protection measures. Adopting a continuous improvement approach ensures that the organization is always prepared to face new threats and adapt to changes in the business and technology environment.

# CHAPTER 10:
# THE FUTURE OF INFORMATION SECURITY

## Trends and Forecasts

The field of information security is constantly evolving, driven by technological advances and changes in cyber threats. For C-Level executives to be prepared for the future, it is essential that they understand the key emerging trends that are shaping the cybersecurity landscape.

**1. Increased Use of Artificial Intelligence and Machine Learning:** Artificial intelligence (AI) and machine learning are revolutionizing the way threats are detected and mitigated. These technologies allow the analysis of large volumes of data in real time, identifying anomalous patterns and behaviors that could go unnoticed by traditional methods.

- **Practical Applications:** Implementing AI systems for continuous monitoring and predictive analysis can improve the ability to detect threats before they cause significant harm. AI-based tools can automate incident response and dynamically adjust security policies based on new information.

**2. Growth of Blockchain Technology:** Blockchain technology is gaining prominence as a solution to ensure transaction integrity and protect data from tampering. The use of blockchain can ensure that records and transactions are transparent and immutable.

- **Practical Applications:** Using blockchain for auditing and data tracking can add an additional layer of security for financial transactions and critical records. Additionally, blockchain can be used to strengthen authentication and integrity of systems and processes.

**3. Expansion of the Internet of Things (IoT):** With the increasing adoption of IoT devices, new attack vectors emerge that need to be managed effectively. Connecting smart devices to corporate networks exposes organizations to additional risks if these devices are not adequately secured.

- **Practical Applications:** Implementing IoT-specific security policies, such as network segmentation and strong authentication, is crucial to protecting devices and data. Additionally, integrating IoT security solutions can monitor and respond to threats specific to these devices.

**4. Remote Work and BYOD (Bring Your Own Device):** The rise of remote work and the use of personal devices for corporate purposes requires new approaches to ensuring security outside traditional perimeters. Device management and data protection in decentralized environments are essential.

- **Practical Applications:** Adopting mobile device management (MDM) solutions and cloud-based security policies can help protect data and maintain compliance with security regulations. Implementing multi-factor authentication and data encryption is also critical to ensuring security in remote work environments.

**Preparing for New Threats**

As cyber threats evolve, organizations must take a proactive stance to prepare for emerging challenges. Here are some approaches to staying ahead of threats:

**1. Implementation of Continuous Threat Assessment Programs:** Conducting regular threat assessments allows you to identify and address vulnerabilities before they can be exploited by attackers. These programs should include attack simulations, risk assessments, and impact analyses.

- **Practical Applications:** Establish a schedule for regular threat and vulnerability assessments, and use pen testing tools and techniques to simulate attacks and test the robustness of defenses.

**2. Regular Update of Cyber Defenses:** Keeping cyber defenses up to date is essential to face new threats. This includes applying software patches and updates, as well as adopting new security technologies.

- **Practical Applications:** Implement a patch management strategy to ensure all security updates are applied in a timely manner. Additionally, regularly review and update security policies and controls to reflect new threats and vulnerabilities.

**3. Investment in Threat Intelligence and Partnerships:** Investing in threat intelligence allows you to access information about new threats and emerging trends. Forming partnerships with other companies and security organizations can also provide valuable insights and improve incident response capabilities.

- **Practical Applications:** Subscribe to threat intelligence feeds and participate in cybersecurity groups and forums to exchange information about threats and best practices. Collaborate with other organizations to share security information and resources.

**4. Creating an Agile and Adaptive Security Environment:** The ability to adapt quickly is essential to face emerging threats. An agile security environment allows you to quickly adjust security strategies and controls as needed.

- **Practical Applications:** Establish a flexible security governance structure and adopt agile development practices to quickly incorporate improvements and adjustments to security strategies.

# Innovations and Opportunities

Technological innovation offers opportunities to strengthen information security and improve defenses against cyber threats. The following innovations are particularly promising:

**1. Advanced Multi-Factor Authentication:** Advanced multi-factor authentication (MFA) provides an additional layer of security by requiring multiple verification methods before granting access to sensitive systems and data.

- **Practical Applications:** Implement MFA solutions that integrate biometrics, hardware tokens, and risk-based authentication to increase the security of critical access and reduce the risk of compromised credentials.

**2. Quantum Cryptography:** Quantum cryptography promises to revolutionize data protection with encryption techniques based on quantum mechanics, which offer much greater security compared to traditional methods.

- **Practical Applications:** Explore the feasibility of quantum cryptography to protect sensitive data and ensure communications security in high-security environments.

**3. Security Automation and Orchestration:** Security automation and orchestration help reduce manual workload and enable faster, more accurate response to security incidents.

- **Practical Applications:** Adopt automation solutions for repetitive tasks and incident response processes. Use orchestration platforms to integrate different security tools and coordinate responses to threats.

**Conclusion**

The future of information security is shaped by technological advances and changes in cyber threats. Being aware of emerging trends, preparing for new threats, and exploring innovations can help organizations maintain a robust and adaptive security posture. Continuous adaptation and adoption of new technologies are essential to protect information assets and ensure security in a constantly evolving environment.

# Conclusion

## Summary of Key Points

This book provided a comprehensive overview of information security, highlighting the importance of active involvement by C-Level executives in protecting the organization's digital and physical assets. Throughout the chapters, we explore the following fundamental aspects:

1. **Definition and Scope of Information Security:** Information security is a set of practices and strategies designed to protect data against unauthorized access, use, disclosure, interruption, modification or destruction. This concept encompasses both digital and physical information, and is crucial to maintaining data confidentiality, integrity and availability.
2. **Main Threats and Vulnerabilities:** We discuss the various threats to information security, which can be

internal or external, including malware, ransomware, phishing, corporate espionage, and software vulnerabilities. Understanding these threats is essential to developing adequate defenses.

3. **C-Level Responsibilities and Involvement:** C-Level executives, such as CEOs, CFOs and CIOs, are responsible for ensuring that information security is a priority in the organization. They must actively participate in formulating security policies and resource allocation.

4. **Corporate Security Culture:** Creating and maintaining a security culture involves promoting behaviors that prioritize data protection at all levels of the organization. This requires exemplary leadership and constant communication.

5. **Policies and Governance:** Well-defined security policies are essential to protect information assets. Governance frameworks, such as ISO 27001 and NIST, provide structures that help ensure security practices are aligned with international standards and best practices.

6. **Risk Management:** Risk management involves identifying, assessing and mitigating potential risks. Business continuity and disaster recovery plans are critical to ensuring continued operation during and after a crisis.

7. **Security Implementation Strategies:** Technologies such as firewalls, intrusion detection systems, and encryption are essential to a robust security strategy. Integrating security into business processes and protecting cloud environments is also crucial.

8. **Security and Innovation:** Digital transformation and the adoption of new technologies, such as IoT, AI and blockchain, bring new challenges and opportunities. Adopting innovative security practices and staying up to date on new technologies is vital to protecting technological innovations.

9. **Communication and Training:** Involving employees

and implementing training and awareness programs are essential to maintaining information security. Effective communication about the importance of security helps ensure buy-in from all levels of the organization.

10. **Incident Response and Crisis Management:** A well-defined incident response plan and specialized crisis response teams are essential to minimizing damage and recovering quickly after a security incident.

11. **Measuring Success:** Measuring the success of security initiatives through KPIs, reports and security audits is crucial to evaluating the effectiveness of practices and identifying areas for improvement.

12. **The Future of Information Security:** Emerging trends, such as the use of AI and machine learning, the expansion of IoT, and remote work, require continuous preparation and adoption of new technologies to face future threats.

# Call to Action for C-Level

C-Level executives play a vital role in protecting their organizations' information assets. This book serves as a guide to better understand your responsibilities and implement effective security practices. It is essential that leaders take concrete steps to integrate information security into their corporate strategies, allocate adequate resources and foster a culture of security at all levels of the organization. Security should not be seen as an isolated task, but as a fundamental aspect of business strategy.

# Final Thoughts

Information security is a continuous and dynamic journey, full of challenges and opportunities. As threats evolve and technologies advance, organizations must remain vigilant and adaptable. The role of the C-Level is fundamental to leading this journey, ensuring that information security is a strategic priority and an integral part of the organizational culture. With the knowledge and tools presented in this book, executives are well prepared to face the security challenges of today and tomorrow. Adopting a proactive and adaptive stance will allow companies to protect their assets, maintain stakeholder trust and ensure sustainable and secure growth.

# Case Study 1: The Extortion Attempt and Effective Resolution

## Case Context

Our company recently came across a sophisticated extortion attempt that was disguised as offering security services. The scenario involved an individual who posed as a cybersecurity expert and claimed to have discovered a critical flaw in our system. This individual offered a service to fix the supposed vulnerability, but the real intention was to extort the company.

## Development of the Situation

The attacker made an initial proposal to sell a service worth twenty thousand reais, claiming that this amount would cover the correction of the flaw he had identified. However, a preliminary analysis of the proposal revealed that the true objective was not to offer a legitimate service, but rather to extort money from the company. The threats included the disclosure of confidential company information, which required a strategic and well-planned response.

To deal with the situation, our team developed a tactical strategy. We created a fictitious scenario in which a company employee, named "João," would contact the attacker. The approach involved creating the impression that the company was interested in its service and willing to negotiate a deal.

# Interaction with the Attacker

During interactions with the attacker, it became clear that he was employing manipulative tactics and did not possess the technical knowledge he claimed. He mentioned the threat of infecting the company's entire network with a virus called "Hansonware," but as he detailed his intentions and methods, it became clear that he did not adequately understand how this type of attack worked. This discrepancy revealed that their threats were unfounded and therefore less concerning than they initially appeared.

# Resolution and Additional Measures

Based on the information gathered and assessment of the situation, our team decided to implement an additional approach to defuse the extortion attempt. We offered the attacker the ability to participate in a vulnerability bounty program, where they could be rewarded based on the criticality of the reported flaws. To participate, the attacker needed to sign a contract and undergo a facial scan.

This strategy had multiple objectives. First, it diverted the attacker's focus, creating the impression that his offer was being seriously considered. Second, by requiring a contract to be signed and a facial scan to be performed, we ensure that any subsequent information leak would result in legal liability for the attacker. The attacker accepted the proposal, mistakenly believing that he was protected and would receive compensation.

However, after the contract was signed, there were no reports of failures or confidential information disclosed. The attacker did not provide any additional details about vulnerabilities, and the situation was closed without further complications.

## Lessons Learned and Safety Measures

After the incident, our company took several measures to reinforce security and avoid future similar problems:

1. **Development of a New Security Policy:** We have implemented a more robust security policy, with clear guidelines for dealing with threats and extortion. The policy includes procedures for verifying the authenticity of offers and reporting vulnerabilities.
2. **Establishment of Security Structure:** We created an organized structure to manage security across different zones of the company, including implementing more stringent protective measures and creating a protocol to address threats and extortion attempts.
3. **Training and Awareness:** We have introduced regular training programs for staff on how to identify and respond to extortion attempts and other types of cyber threats.

## Conclusion

This case illustrates the importance of a strategic and well-planned response to dealing with extortion attempts. The approach taken not only prevented a potential attack, but also strengthened our security practices, better preparing the company to face future challenges. The situation demonstrated that a well-designed strategy can disarm extortion attempts and protect the integrity of the organization, highlighting the need for proactive measures and a solid security posture.

# Case Study 2: Strengthening Security and Corporate Image through a Pentest

## Company Context

Company X, a prominent organization in the technology and Software as a Service (SaaS) sector, recognized the critical importance of cybersecurity to the company's operation and reputation. In an increasingly competitive market, the company not only wanted to improve its information security posture, but also reinforce its image of trust with customers and partners. With growing concerns about data protection and the integrity of operations, the company decided to carry out a comprehensive pen test to identify and correct possible vulnerabilities.

## Challenges and Objectives

The main objective of the pen test was to detect vulnerabilities in the company's systems, networks and internal processes, and subsequently implement necessary corrections to strengthen security. In addition to protecting sensitive data and ensuring operational integrity, company X also aimed to improve its market image, demonstrating its commitment to the security and protection of customer data.

# Challenges faced:

- Identification and correction of critical vulnerabilities.
- Update of security practices and policies.
- Strengthening the trust of customers and partners.

**Main objectives:**

- Identify vulnerabilities and weaknesses in IT infrastructure.
- Implement corrective measures to improve security.
- Improve the company's perception in the market regarding its security posture.

**Pentest execution**

Company X hired a team of cybersecurity experts to conduct the pentest. The process was meticulously planned and executed, covering several phases:

1. **Planning and Scope:** The pentest team defined the scope of the test, including which systems, networks, and applications would be analyzed. This phase included prior agreements with the company on the objectives and limits of the pentest.
2. **Recognition and Information Collection:** The team began collecting information about the company's IT infrastructure, using passive and active reconnaissance techniques to map systems and identify possible attack vectors.
3. **Vulnerability Exploitation:** Real attacks were simulated to exploit identified vulnerabilities. This included penetration testing of networks, authentication systems

and web applications, among others.

4. **Analysis and Report:** The team documented the findings, classified the vulnerabilities based on their severity and potential impact, and provided a detailed report with recommendations for mitigation.

During the pen test, several security flaws were identified, including:

- **Critical Vulnerabilities in Authentication Systems:** Faults that could allow unauthorized access to systems.
- **Inadequate Network Configuration:** Weaknesses in security configurations that could be exploited by attackers.
- **Sensitive Data Exposures:** Sensitive data inadvertently exposed, increasing the risk of leaks.

### Corrective Actions and Security Improvement

Based on the pentest report, Company X implemented a series of corrective measures and improved its security posture:

1. **Vulnerability Fix:** All identified flaws have been addressed. Actions included updating systems, reviewing security configurations and strengthening authentication measures. Critical vulnerabilities have been patched as a priority.
2. **Strengthening Security Policies:** The company's security policies have been reviewed and updated to align with current best practices and regulations. New guidelines have been established to ensure ongoing compliance and adequate data protection.
3. **Team Training:** Intensive training was carried out for employees, focusing on security practices, awareness of cyber threats and the importance of adhering to new security policies. This training helped create a more robust security culture within the organization.

### Impact on Image and Trust

Carrying out the pen test and subsequent correction of the vulnerabilities resulted in several tangible benefits for company X:

1. **Increased Customer Confidence:** The company was able to proactively demonstrate its commitment to security, which resulted in an increase in customer confidence and loyalty. Customers began to see the company as a responsible and trustworthy organization in protecting their data.

2. **Differentiation in the Market:** The company stood out in the market as a proactive organization in cybersecurity. This helped attract new customers and strengthen existing partnerships, differentiating the company from the competition.

3. **Preparation for Audits and Compliance:** By improving security practices and updating policies, the company was better prepared for audits and compliance with security regulations. This preparation made it easier to obtain certifications and comply with regulatory requirements, further strengthening the company's position in the market.

## Conclusion

The pen test carried out by company X was a decisive step towards identifying and correcting critical vulnerabilities and improving information security. In addition to strengthening internal security, pen testing provided significant benefits in terms of corporate image and customer trust. The proactive approach taken not only strengthened the company's defenses, but also positioned it as a security leader in the technology and SaaS sector. This case study exemplifies how information security can be an important strategic advantage, contributing to a company's sustainable growth and positive reputation.

# CYBERSECURITY CHECKLIST FOR MANAGERS

In the current scenario, where cyber threats evolve rapidly and data protection becomes increasingly critical, it is imperative that business managers adopt a structured and comprehensive approach to cybersecurity. THE **Cybersecurity Checklist for Managers** is designed to serve as a valuable tool in assessing and improving your organization's security posture.

**Checklist Objective:** The main objective of this checklist is to help you map your business's current cybersecurity situation and identify areas that require immediate attention. By executing this checklist, you will be able to assess the strengths and weaknesses of your security infrastructure, in addition to creating an effective implementation plan, prioritizing the most achievable and impactful actions.

**Implementation Strategy:** To make the implementation of the actions listed more efficient, we suggest that you develop a detailed plan, measuring the time and investment needed to complete each step of the checklist. This approach will not only help ensure that resources are allocated effectively, but will also allow you to continually monitor progress and make adjustments as necessary. Consider using a timeline and budget table to track milestones and associated costs.

**Additional Tips:**

1. **Continuous Assessment:** Carry out periodic reviews of your security posture to ensure that the measures adopted remain effective and up to date in the face of new threats.
2. **Stakeholder Involvement:** Involve your organization's key stakeholders in the security process. Top management buy-in and engagement from all areas are crucial to the success of security initiatives.
3. **Qualification and Training:** Invest in ongoing training for your team to ensure everyone is aware of security best practices and prepared to identify and respond to threats.
4. **Documentation and Registration:** Maintain detailed documentation of all measures implemented and analyzes performed. This not only helps you keep track of progress, but is also essential for future audits and reviews.
5. **Adaptation to Changes:** Be prepared to adapt your security strategies based on technological changes and new emerging threats. Cybersecurity is a dynamic field that requires continuous flexibility and innovation.

Using this checklist as an integral part of your strategic planning will enable a systematic and effective approach to protecting your organization's digital assets, contributing to a robust and resilient security posture.

# 1. Governance and Security Policies

- **Develop and Implement an Information Security Policy:**
    - Clearly define expectations and responsibilities regarding information security.

- Include specific guidelines on access control, acceptable use, protecting sensitive data, and incident response.
- Establish a process for periodically reviewing and updating the policy.
- Conduct training workshops to ensure all employees understand and comply with the policy.

- **Establish a Governance Framework, such as ISO 27001 or NIST:**
  - Adopt a governance framework, such as ISO 27001 or NIST, to structure security practices and processes.
  - Conduct an initial assessment to identify gaps in the chosen framework and develop an action plan to implement the recommended controls.
  - Establish a process for regular internal reviews and audits to ensure ongoing compliance with the framework.

- **Ensure Compliance with Applicable Regulations and Laws (GDPR, CCPA, etc.):**
  - Stay up to date on local and international regulations and adapt your policies as needed.
  - Develop and implement specific policies and procedures to ensure compliance with data protection laws such as GDPR and CCPA.
  - Conduct regular compliance audits to identify and correct any non-conformities.
  - Maintain detailed compliance records and prepare for external audits and regulatory inspections.

- **Create and Regularly Review Security Procedures and Protocols:**
  - Document detailed procedures for security operations, including incident management and access control.
  - Regularly review and update these procedures to reflect changes in the company's threat environment, technology, and operations.
  - Conduct post-incident reviews to identify and

implement procedural improvements.

# 2. Risk Assessment and Management

- **Conduct a Comprehensive Risk Assessment:**
  - Use methodologies such as business impact analysis (BIA) and qualitative and quantitative risk analysis.
  - Engage cross-functional teams to gain a complete view of risks and assess potential impacts across all areas of the organization.
  - Document and prioritize identified risks based on likelihood and impact.
- **Implement Mitigation Measures for Identified Risks:**
  - Develop specific mitigation plans for identified risks, including technical controls, operational adjustments and administrative measures.
  - Implement security controls, such as firewalls and encryption, to protect against identified risks.
  - Monitor the effectiveness of mitigation measures and adjust as necessary.
- **Develop and Maintain a Business Continuity Plan:**
  - Create a comprehensive business continuity plan (BCP) that includes strategies for maintaining critical operations and communicating with stakeholders during disruptions.
  - Perform regular testing of the BCP to ensure it is effective and make adjustments as needed.
- **Establish a Disaster Recovery Plan and Test It Periodically:**
  - Develop a disaster recovery plan (DRP) that defines procedures for restoring systems and data after a catastrophic event.
  - Perform regular DRP testing to ensure recovery

processes are effective and update the plan based on test results.

# 3. Data and Information Security

- **Implement Need-Based and Authorization Access Controls:**
  - Use access controls based on the principle of least privilege, granting access only to information necessary to perform specific functions.
  - Implement multi-factor authentication (MFA) to enforce access control.
  - Regularly review access permissions and adjust as employees' roles change.
- **Ensuring Data Encryption in Transit and at Rest:**
  - Use strong encryption to protect data during transmission and when stored on devices.
  - Maintain the security of encryption keys and implement secure key management practices.
  - Perform regular audits to verify the effectiveness of encryption measures.
- **Establish Data Backup and Recovery Processes:**
  - Implement a backup strategy that includes regular, secure backups of critical data, both on-premises and in the cloud.
  - Test recovery processes to ensure that backups can be restored effectively in the event of data loss.
  - Use integrity checking tools to ensure that backups are not corrupted.
- **Monitor and Protect Data Against Leaks and Unauthorized Access:**
  - Utilize monitoring tools and data loss prevention (DLP) solutions to detect and prevent data leaks and

unauthorized access.
- o        Implement policies and procedures to detect suspicious activity and quickly respond to incidents.

# 4. IT and Infrastructure Security

- **Implement and Maintain Firewalls and Intrusion Detection Systems (IDS/IPS):**
  - o Configure firewalls to filter network traffic and prevent unauthorized access.
  - o Use intrusion detection and prevention systems (IDS/IPS) to identify and respond to malicious activity on the network.
  - o Regularly update IDS/IPS signatures to detect the latest threats.
- **Perform Regular Updates and Patches for Systems and Software:**
  - o Keep all systems and software updated with the latest security patches.
  - o Implement a patch management process that includes assessment, testing, and patching.
  - o Monitor and report security vulnerabilities and proactively apply patches.
- **Implement Antivirus and Antimalware Solutions:**
  - o Install and regularly update antivirus and antimalware solutions to protect against viruses, worms, and other threats.
  - o Perform regular system scans and keep antivirus definitions up to date.
- **Ensure the Security of Internal and External Networks:**
  - o Protect internal and external networks with appropriate security measures, such as network segmentation and access point protection.

o        Use VPNs to ensure the security of remote connections and implement continuous monitoring to identify potential threats.

o        Conduct regular security assessments to verify the effectiveness of network protection measures.

# 5. Training and Awareness

- **Develop and Implement Safety Training Programs for Employees:**
  - o    Create and implement training programs that include topics such as security best practices, company policies, and how to identify and respond to threats.
  - o        Conduct regular and mandatory training for all employees and offer refresher modules.
  - o    Provide ongoing support materials and resources to help employees stay up to date.
- **Conduct Cyber Threat Awareness Campaigns:**
  - o    Implement awareness campaigns that address current cyber threats such as phishing, social engineering, and ransomware.
  - o        Use emails, workshops, seminars and attack simulations to educate employees.
  - o    Promote awareness through quizzes and assessments to reinforce learning.
- **Evaluate the Effectiveness of Training Programs Regularly:**
  - o      Monitor and evaluate the effectiveness of training and awareness programs using testing, research, and incident analysis.
  - o        Collects feedback from participants and adjusts programs based on identified needs.
  - o        Conduct attack simulations, such as phishing, to

test and reinforce employees' ability to recognize and respond to threats.

# 6. Incident Response and Crisis Management

- **Create and Maintain an Incident Response Plan:**
  - Develop a detailed plan that includes procedures to identify, contain, eradicate, and recover from security incidents.
  - Establish an internal and external communication process during an incident.
  - Update the plan based on lessons learned from previous incidents and conduct periodic reviews.
- **Establish and Train an Incident Response Team (CSIRT):**
  - Form a team dedicated to incident response, including experts in various areas of security.
  - Conduct regular training and drills to ensure staff are prepared to deal with different types of incidents.
  - Keep staff informed about the latest threats and response techniques.
- **Develop Communication Procedures for Crises and Data Leaks:**
  - Create clear procedures for communicating with all stakeholders, including customers, partners and authorities, during a crisis.
  - Establish protocols for reporting data breaches and other occurrences in a transparent and timely manner.
  - Prepare standard statements and communications for common situations and customize as needed.
- **Review and Update Incident Response Plans After Events:**
  - After an incident, conduct a detailed analysis to identify lessons learned and areas for improvement.

- ○ Update the incident response plan based on findings from post-incident analysis.
- ○ Hold review meetings to share learnings and adjust response strategies.

# 7. Monitoring and Auditing

- **Implement Continuous Monitoring of Systems and Networks:**
  - ○ Use monitoring tools to track activity in real time and detect potential threats.
  - ○ Establish alerts for suspicious activity and set up automatic analysis to identify attack patterns.
  - ○ Maintain detailed event and access logs for analysis and incident response.
- **Conduct Regular Security and Compliance Audits:**
  - ○ Conduct internal and external audits to verify the effectiveness of security measures and compliance with policies and regulations.
  - ○ Prepare for compliance audits with required documentation and respond to any issues identified.
  - ○ Use audit results to continually improve security practices.
- **Analyze and Report Security Metrics and Performance Indicators (KPIs):**
  - ○ Define and monitor security-related KPIs such as number of incidents detected, response time, and effectiveness of mitigation measures.
  - ○ Analyze metrics reports to identify trends and areas for improvement.
  - ○ Present safety performance reports to senior management and use the data to support strategic decisions.

# 8. Application and Systems Security

- **Perform Penetration Testing and Security Assessments on Applications:**
  - Conduct regular penetration tests to identify and fix vulnerabilities in applications and systems.
  - Use automated and manual tools to perform security assessments and identify weaknesses.
  - Implement fixes and improvements based on test results.
- **Implement Secure Development Practices (DevSecOps):**
  - Integrate security practices into the software development lifecycle, from design to implementation and maintenance.
  - Use the DevSecOps methodology to promote collaboration between development, operations and security teams.
  - Perform code reviews to identify and fix vulnerabilities and make use of code security analysis tools.
- **Manage and Protect the Lifecycle of Applications and Systems:**
  - Adopt practices to manage security during the development, implementation, maintenance and retirement of applications and systems.
  - Implement security controls, such as strong authentication and encryption, during all phases of the lifecycle.
  - Establish procedures to safely decommission and remove obsolete systems and associated data.
- **Utilizar CAPTCHA e Web Application Firewall (WAF):**
  - Implement CAPTCHA to protect forms and other inputs from bots and automated attacks.
  - Use a Web Application Firewall (WAF) to protect

web applications against common attacks such as SQL injections and cross-site scripting (XSS).

- o    Perform regular adjustments and updates to WAF configurations to ensure ongoing protection.
- **Sanitizing User Inputs:**
  - o    Implement user input sanitization and validation practices to prevent injection attacks and other vulnerabilities.
  - o    Use secure libraries and frameworks to handle data input and prevent the execution of malicious code.
  - o    Perform regular reviews and testing to ensure input sanitization is being applied correctly.

# 9. Security in Cloud and Hybrid Environments

- **Implement Specific Security Controls for Cloud Environments:**
  - o    Adopt appropriate security controls for cloud environments, such as data encryption and identity and access management.
  - o    Utilize cloud-native security solutions and third-party tools to protect data and resources.
  - o    Conduct regular security assessments to ensure security practices comply with best practices.
- **Ensuring Data Protection in Hybrid and Multi-Cloud Environments:**
  - o    Develop security policies that integrate and monitor hybrid and multi-cloud environments to ensure consistent protection.
  - o    Utilize security tools that provide visibility and control over all of your cloud instances.
  - o    Conduct regular reviews and assessments to identify

and mitigate risks specific to hybrid and multi-cloud environments.

- **Monitor and Manage Access and Security on Cloud Platforms:**
  - o Implement strict access control and multi-factor authentication policies to protect your cloud accounts and data.
  - o Utilize cloud platform-specific monitoring tools to detect and respond to suspicious activity.
  - o Conduct periodic security audits to ensure security practices are being followed appropriately.

# 10. Innovation and the Future of Security

- **Monitor and Adopt Safe Technological Innovations:**
  - o Stay up to date on the latest technological innovations and assess their impact on security.
  - o Perform risk analyzes for new technologies and adopt them securely, ensuring they do not introduce new vulnerabilities.
  - o Attend events and training to stay ahead of emerging trends and understand security implications.
- **Assess and Prepare for New Security Threats and Trends:**
  - o Perform regular threat analysis to identify new threats and emerging exploitation techniques.
  - o Update your response plans and mitigation strategies to address newly identified threats.
  - o Join security groups and forums to learn about the latest trends and threats.
- **Invest in Emerging Technologies to Strengthen Security Posture:**
  - o Consider investing in emerging technologies, such

as artificial intelligence and blockchain, to improve information security.

o     Assess the feasibility and effectiveness of these technologies in the context of your organization and run pilots to test their impact.

o     Use these technologies to improve threat detection, ensure data integrity, and improve incident response.

# CYBERSECURITY ACTION PLAN FOR MANAGERS

## 1. Governance and Security Policies

### Develop and Implement an Information Security Policy

1. **Creating a Clear and Comprehensive Policy:**
   - **Setting Expectations and Responsibilities:** The information security policy should begin with a clear statement of the expectations and responsibilities of all employees regarding data security. This includes protecting sensitive information, using systems safely, and complying with established standards and procedures. The policy should specify who is responsible for implementing and maintaining security measures, including senior management, the IT department, and employees.
   - **Essential Components:** The policy must cover a number of crucial topics:
     - **Access Control:** Define how access to information will be managed, including granting, reviewing and revoking permissions. Specify the user categories and access levels required for each

role.

- **Acceptable Use:** Establish rules about how systems and data can be used. This may include restrictions on the use of personal devices, rules for sending and receiving emails, and the use of software.
- **Data Protection:** Define how data should be protected, both in transit and at rest. Include guidance on encryption, backup, and secure storage.
- **Incident Response:** Document the procedures to be followed in the event of a security incident. This should include incident identification, notification, containment, eradication and recovery.

o **Stakeholder Involvement:** To ensure that the information security policy addresses the organization's specific needs and risks, it is crucial to involve stakeholders from different departments, such as human resources, legal, finance and operations. This collaborative approach ensures that the policy is comprehensive and applicable to all areas of the company.

2. **Communication and Training:**

o **Policy Disclosure:** After the policy is created, it must be widely disseminated within the organization. This may include distributing copies to all employees, posting on an internal portal, and holding meetings to discuss the policy.

o **Continuous Training:** Host training sessions to educate employees about the details of the policy and the importance of information security. Training must be ongoing, with regular updates to reflect changes in policy and the threat environment.

# Establish a Governance Framework, such as ISO 27001 or NIST

1. **Adopt a Security Governance Framework:**
   o      **ISO 27001:** ISO 27001 offers a systematic approach to managing sensitive information, aiming to protect the confidentiality, integrity and availability of data. The standard requires the implementation of an Information Security Management System (ISMS) that includes defining a scope, carrying out a risk assessment, and implementing security controls and measures. Furthermore, ISO 27001 requires continuous review and improvement of the ISMS, with internal and external audits.

   o      **NIST (National Institute of Standards and Technology):** The NIST framework provides detailed guidelines on cyber protection, helping organizations create a solid foundation for security. The NIST Cybersecurity Framework (CSF) is divided into five main functions: Identify, Protect, Detect, Respond, and Recover. Each function is subdivided into categories and subcategories that detail specific practices and controls. Adopting NIST helps create a flexible framework that can be adapted to meet the specific needs and risks of different organizations.

2. **Benefits of Frameworks:**
   o      **Structure and Consistency:** Adopting frameworks such as ISO 27001 and NIST provides a consistent and comprehensive framework for information security management. This helps ensure that all aspects of security are addressed in an organized and coordinated manner.

   o      **Continuous Improvement:** Both frameworks

promote continuous improvement by encouraging organizations to regularly review and update their security practices in response to changes in the threat environment and business needs.

o   **Recognition and Credibility:** ISO 27001 certification, for example, can improve the organization's credibility and demonstrate to an external audience, including customers and partners, its commitment to information security.

# Ensure Compliance with Applicable Regulations and Laws (GDPR, CCPA, etc.)

1.  **Staying Updated on Regulations:**

o   **Continuous Monitoring:** Compliance with data protection regulations and laws, such as GDPR (General Data Protection Regulation) in Europe and CCPA (California Consumer Privacy Act) in the US, requires continuous monitoring to keep up with changes in laws and regulations. Utilize legal and compliance consulting services to ensure your organization is always compliant.

o   **Impact Analysis:** Conduct regulatory impact analyzes to identify how changes in legislation may affect the organization and its operations. This analysis must consider how the organization collects, stores, processes and shares personal data.

2.  **Develop Compliance Policies and Procedures:**

o   **Data Protection Policies:** Create specific policies to ensure your organization complies with data protection regulations. This may include policies for the handling of personal data, data access requests and data breach notifications.

○ **Compliance Procedures:** Establish clear procedures for the collection, processing and storage of personal data. Include guidance on how to handle data access requests, data deletion, and consent management.

3. **Perform Regular Audits:**

○ **Internal and External Audits:** Conduct regular internal audits to verify compliance with data protection policies and procedures. Additionally, consider conducting external audits to gain an unbiased, independent view of your organization's compliance.

○ **Reports and Corrective Actions:** Document audit results and develop action plans to correct any identified deficiencies. Monitor the implementation of these corrective actions to ensure issues are resolved effectively.

# Create and Regularly Review Security Procedures and Protocols

1. **Detailed Documentation of Security Procedures:**

○ **Creating Procedures:** Document detailed procedures for all security operations, including incident management, access control, and data protection. These documents must clearly describe the steps to be followed, the responsibilities of each party involved and the resources required.

○ **Documentation Maintenance:** Keep documentation updated to reflect changes in processes, technology, and the threat environment. This includes updating existing procedures and adding new procedures as needed.

2. **Regular Review and Update:**

- o  **Periodic Review:** Establish a schedule to regularly review and update security procedures and protocols. Revisions must take into account new risks, changes in legislation and feedback from users and security teams.
- o  **Tests and Simulations:** Conduct tests and simulations to validate the effectiveness of security procedures. This may include penetration testing, incident response simulations, and process reviews to identify areas for improvement.

3. **Feedback and Continuous Improvement:**
- o  **Feedback Collection:** Solicit feedback from users and stakeholders on the effectiveness of security procedures and protocols. Use this feedback to identify areas for improvement and adjust procedures as needed.
- o  **Implementation of Improvements:** Build on test results, audits, and feedback to implement continuous improvements to security procedures. This helps ensure that the organization is always prepared to face new challenges and threats.

# 2. Risk Assessment and Management

## Conduct a Comprehensive Risk Assessment

1. **Identification and Assessment of Potential Risks:**
- o  **Assessment Methodologies:** Use established methodologies to identify and assess potential risks to information security. Business impact analysis (BIA) helps identify which processes and assets are critical to the organization's operation and what the

consequences of their disruption would be. Qualitative and quantitative risk analysis assesses the likelihood and impact of identified risks, enabling a detailed understanding of threats and vulnerabilities.

- **Business Impact Analysis (BIA):** Assess how disruption of different functions and systems would affect the organization, considering financial loss, reputational damage, and impact on regulatory compliance. Identify critical resources and define recovery requirements.
- **Qualitative and Quantitative Risk Analysis:** Use qualitative analysis to classify risks based on their severity and likelihood, and quantitative analysis to measure the financial and operational impact of risks. This may include creating risk scenarios and using modeling tools to predict potential impacts.

2. **Involvement of Cross-Functional Teams:**
   - **Participation of Various Departments:** Engage teams from different departments, such as IT, operations, legal, and finance, to get a comprehensive view of risks. Each department can identify specific risks related to their areas of activity and provide valuable information about the possible risk implications for their operations.
   - **Risk Workshops and Meetings:** Organize regular workshops and meetings with cross-functional teams to discuss identified risks and assess priorities. Use brainstorming techniques and SWOT analysis (Strengths, Weaknesses, Opportunities and Threats) to generate a complete view of the risks facing the organization.

# Implement Mitigation Measures

# for Identified Risks

1. **Development and Implementation of Mitigation Plans:**
   o **Creation of Mitigation Plans:** Develop detailed mitigation plans to reduce or eliminate identified risks. These plans must include technical, operational and administrative measures to address each risk. Measures may involve the implementation of technical controls, such as firewalls and encryption, adjustments to operational processes, such as reviews of procedures and protocols, and the adoption of administrative measures, such as policies and training.
     - **Technical Controls:** Install and maintain appropriate technical controls to protect systems and data. This may include applying security patches, configuring intrusion detection and prevention systems, and using encryption to protect sensitive data.
     - **Operational Adjustments:** Reevaluate and adjust operational processes to reduce risks. This may involve reviewing work procedures, implementing stricter access controls and carrying out internal audits to identify areas for improvement.
     - **Administrative Measures:** Develop policies and procedures to manage risk and train employees to ensure everyone is aware of security practices and compliance requirements.
2. **Prioritization of Actions:**
   o **Risk Criticality Assessment:** Prioritize mitigation actions based on the criticality of identified risks and available resources. Risks that have a high potential impact and high probability of occurrence should receive greater attention and resources for mitigation.
   o **Resource Allocation:** Align resource allocation with established priorities. This may involve allocating

budget, personnel and technology to areas of highest risk and continually monitoring the effectiveness of implemented measures.

# Develop and Maintain a Business Continuity Plan

1. **Preparation of the Business Continuity Plan (BCP):**
   o **Creation of the BCP:** Develop a business continuity plan (BCP) to ensure the organization can continue operating in the event of significant disruptions. The BCP must identify critical business processes, establish procedures to maintain the continuity of operations and define strategies for recovery.
      ▪ **Strategies for Maintaining Critical Operations:** Define strategies to maintain continuity of essential operations during an outage. This may include implementing backup solutions, establishing alternative work locations, and coordinating with suppliers and partners.
      ▪ **Communication with Stakeholders:** Develop a communications plan that ensures all stakeholders, including employees, customers, and partners, are adequately informed during an outage. Establish communication channels and protocols to ensure effective and timely communication.
2. **BCP Maintenance and Update:**
   o **Regular Reviews:** Review and update the BCP regularly to reflect changes in the organization, the threat environment, and business continuity best practices. This includes updating contact information, recovery procedures, and mitigation strategies.

- ○ **Trainings and Simulations:** Conduct regular training and simulations to ensure all employees are familiar with BCP and know how to respond to an outage. Use these trainings to test and validate the effectiveness of the plan and make adjustments as needed.

# Establish a Disaster Recovery Plan and Test It Periodically

1. **Creation of the Disaster Recovery Plan (DRP):**
- ○ **DRP development:** Create a disaster recovery plan (DRP) that defines how the organization will restore its systems and data after a catastrophic event. The DRP must include procedures for recovering data, restoring systems, and resuming normal operations.
  - **Recovery Procedures:** Establish detailed procedures for recovering data and systems, including recovering backups, restoring applications, and validating data integrity.
  - **Designation of Responsibilities:** Define the responsibilities and roles of the disaster recovery team, including coordinating recovery activities and communicating with stakeholders.
2. **Regular DRP Tests:**
- ○ **Testing:** Conduct regular testing of the DRP to ensure the plan is effective and that all procedures work as expected. Testing may include disaster simulations and recovery exercises to assess the organization's readiness and response capacity.
- ○ **Review and Adjustments:** After testing, review the DRP to identify areas for improvement and make any necessary adjustments. Document test results and lessons learned to refine the plan and improve

responsiveness to future disasters.

# 3. Data and Information Security

## Implement Need-Based and Authorization Access Controls

1. **Establishment of Access Controls:**
   o **Definition of Access Policies:** Develop access control policies that clearly define who is allowed to access what data and resources. Policies should detail authorization requirements for access, authentication methods, and processes for granting and revoking access.
   o **Role-Based Access Control (RBAC):** Implement the role-based access control (RBAC) model, where access rights are assigned based on the roles played by users in the organization. This ensures that employees only have access to the information necessary for their specific functions, minimizing the risk of unauthorized access.
   o **Principle of Least Privilege:** Adopt the principle of least privilege, giving users the minimum access necessary to perform their tasks. This reduces the attack surface and limits the possibility of exploiting sensitive data.
2. **Identity and Access Management (IAM):**
   o **IAM Tools:** Use identity and access management (IAM) solutions to automate and control access to systems and data. IAM tools help manage authentication, authorization and access auditing in a centralized and efficient way.
   o **Regular Reviews and Audits:** Perform periodic reviews

of access rights to ensure they are aligned with users' current roles. Conduct audits to identify and correct any discrepancies or unauthorized access.

# Ensuring Data Encryption in Transit and at Rest

1.  **Data Encryption in Transit:**
    o   **Secure Protocols:** Use strong encryption protocols, such as TLS (Transport Layer Security), to protect data while it is being transmitted over the network. Data encryption in transit prevents sensitive information from being intercepted and read by unauthorized third parties.
    o   **Digital Certificates:** Implement digital certificates to authenticate and encrypt communications between servers and clients. SSL/TLS certificates are essential to ensure the security of online transactions and the protection of transmitted data.
2.  **Data Encryption at Rest:**
    o   **Storage Encryption:** Protect data stored on devices and servers using disk encryption. Encryption at rest ensures that even if the device is compromised, the data remains inaccessible without the appropriate decryption keys.
    o   **Algorithms and Keys:** Use strong encryption algorithms such as AES (Advanced Encryption Standard) with appropriately sized keys. Keep encryption keys secure by implementing strict access controls and secure key rotation and storage procedures.

# Establish Data Backup and Recovery Processes

1. **Backup Strategy:**
   - **Backup Types:** Implement a backup strategy that includes full, differential, and incremental backups. This ensures efficient data recovery, minimizing loss in the event of failure or disaster.
   - **Safe Storage:** Store backups in secure locations separate from the main infrastructure, such as in different physical locations or in the cloud. Use encryption to protect stored backups and ensure data confidentiality.
2. **Testing and Validation of Recovery Processes:**
   - **Regular Tests:** Perform data recovery tests to verify the integrity and effectiveness of backups. Tests must simulate data loss scenarios and ensure that backups can be restored effectively and within established deadlines.
   - **Recovery Plans:** Develop and maintain data recovery plans that define procedures for restoring data in different disaster scenarios. Include steps to verify the integrity of recovered data and ensure continuity of operations.

# Monitor and Protect Data against Leaks and Unauthorized Access

1. **Data Monitoring Tools:**
   - **Real-Time Monitoring:** Use monitoring tools to

continually monitor data access and usage. Monitoring solutions help identify and respond to suspicious activity, such as unauthorized access or attempted data leaks.

- o **Log Analysis:** Implement systems for collecting and analyzing access logs and security events. Log analysis enables early detection of anomalous behavior and investigation of security incidents.

2. **Data Loss Prevention (DLP) Solutions:**

- o **DLP implementation:** Adopt data loss prevention (DLP) solutions to identify, monitor, and protect sensitive data from accidental or malicious leaks. DLP tools can apply security policies to control movement and access to critical data.
- o **Policies and Settings:** Configure DLP policies to protect data in different states, such as in transit, at rest, and in use. Establish rules for classifying data and applying controls based on the organization's specific needs and risks.

3. **Continuous Monitoring:**

- o **Risk Assessment:** Conduct ongoing assessments of the risks associated with data and information to ensure that protective measures remain effective. Regularly review and adjust monitoring and protection strategies to address new threats and emerging vulnerabilities.
- o **Incident Response:** Establish processes for responding to data-related incidents, including breach notification and impact mitigation. Develop plans to manage and investigate data security incidents and implement corrective measures to prevent future events.

Implementing these data and information security practices will help protect the confidentiality, integrity, and availability of your organization's critical data, ensuring a robust and resilient security posture.

# 4. IT and Infrastructure Security

## Implement and Maintain Firewalls and Intrusion Detection Systems (IDS/IPS)

1. **Firewalls:**
   o **Configuration and Implementation:** Implement firewalls at network perimeters and between different security zones within the organization. Configure firewall rules and policies to control inbound and outbound traffic, ensuring that only authorized traffic can pass through the firewall.
   o **Next Generation Firewall (NGFW):** Consider adopting next-generation firewalls (NGFW), which offer advanced functionality such as deep packet inspection (DPI), application filtering, and integration with intrusion prevention systems (IPS).
   o **Monitoring and Adjustments:** Monitor firewall performance and adjust your firewall rules as needed to handle new types of traffic and emerging threats. Perform regular reviews of firewall rules to ensure they are up to date and aligned with your organization's security policies.
2. **Intrusion Detection and Prevention Systems (IDS/IPS):**
   o **IDS/IPS implementation:** Install intrusion detection systems (IDS) to identify suspicious activity and potential intrusions, and intrusion prevention systems (IPS) to respond to and block attacks in real time. Configure systems to monitor network traffic and generate alerts about anomalous activity.
   o **Subscriptions and Rules Update:** Keep IDS/

IPS signatures and rules up to date to ensure systems can detect and respond to the latest threats. Regular updates are essential to maintain the effectiveness of IDS/IPS solutions.

- o   **Incident Analysis and Response:** Use data generated by IDS/IPS to investigate and respond to security incidents. Establish procedures to analyze alerts, determine the severity of incidents, and take corrective action to mitigate impacts.

# Perform Regular Updates and Patches for Systems and Software

1. **Patch Management:**
   - o   **Systems and Software Inventory:** Maintain a detailed inventory of all systems and software in use within the organization. This helps identify which systems need updates and patches.
   - o   **Update Cycle:** Establish a regular cycle for applying security patches and updates. This includes monitoring vendor updates, compatibility testing, and deploying patches in a controlled environment before widespread application.
2. **Vulnerability Assessment:**
   - o   **Vulnerability Scan:** Perform vulnerability scans to identify known security holes in systems and software. Use vulnerability assessment tools to detect and prioritize the risks associated with these flaws.
   - o   **Correction and Verification:** Apply fixes and patches for identified vulnerabilities and verify that updates have been applied successfully. Document the remediation process and keep records of updates made.

# Implement Antivirus and Antimalware Solutions

1. **Antivirus and Antimalware Solutions:**
   - **Installation and Configuration:** Install antivirus and antimalware solutions on all systems in your organization, including servers, workstations, and mobile devices. Configure solutions to perform regular, real-time scans.
   - **Subscription Updates:** Keep virus and malware signatures up to date to ensure solutions can identify and neutralize the latest threats. Configure automatic updates to ensure definitions are always up to date.
2. **Regular Scans and Incident Resolution:**
   - **Regular Scans:** Schedule regular scans to identify and remove malware on systems. Perform periodic full scans to ensure the system is free of threats and maintains a secure environment.
   - **Malware Resolution:** Develop procedures to deal with malware infections. This includes quarantining suspicious files, removing malware, and performing post-incident analysis to identify the source and extent of the infection.

# Ensure the Security of Internal and External Networks

1. **Internal Network Security:**
   - **Network Segmentation:** Implement network segmentation to isolate different areas of the network,

reducing the risk of attacks propagating. Use VLANs (Virtual Local Area Networks) and security zones to control traffic between network segments.

o **Network Access Control:** Utilize network access controls (NAC) to ensure that only authorized and secure devices can connect to the internal network. Verify devices' compliance with security policies before allowing access.

2. **External Network Security:**

o **Access Point Protection:** Protect network access points, such as routers and switches, using strong authentication, encryption, and appropriate security configurations. Perform regular configuration reviews to identify and fix vulnerabilities.

o **VPNs and Remote Connections:** Use virtual private networks (VPNs) to ensure the security of remote connections. VPNs encrypt data traffic and ensure that communications between remote employees and the corporate network are secure.

o **Network Monitoring:** Implement monitoring tools to monitor network activity, identify suspicious traffic, and detect potential threats. Use traffic analysis systems to identify anomalous patterns and quickly respond to security incidents.

Implementing and maintaining these security practices for IT and infrastructure helps protect the organization against a wide range of cyber threats, ensuring the integrity, confidentiality and availability of critical systems and data.

# 5. Training and Awareness

## Develop and Implement Safety

# Training Programs for Employees

1. **Creation of Training Programs:**
   - **Training Content:** Develop training programs that cover fundamental aspects of information security, such as protecting personal and corporate data, identifying phishing and other cyber threats, and enforcing the organization's security policies. Include practical examples and real-life scenarios to facilitate understanding.
   - **Training Format:** Use a variety of formats to suit different learning styles, such as in-person training, e-learning modules, instructional videos, and case studies. Ensure content is accessible and engaging to maximize participation and knowledge retention.
2. **Implementation and Update:**
   - **Training Schedule:** Establish a regular schedule for safety training, including orientation sessions for new employees and refresher training for existing staff. Adjust frequency based on your organization's needs and risk level.
   - **Feedback and Continuous Improvement:** Collects feedback from participants on the relevance and effectiveness of training. Use this information to continually improve the content and format of programs, ensuring they are aligned with the latest practices and needs of the organization.

# Conduct Cyber Threat Awareness Campaigns

1. **Campaign Development:**

- o **Themes and Messages:** Create awareness campaigns that address specific cyber threats, such as ransomware, phishing, social engineering, and data breaches. Develop clear, direct messages to educate employees about risks and best practices to mitigate them.
- o **Communication Channels:** Use multiple channels to disseminate information, such as emails, newsletters, bulletin boards, workshops, and seminars. Consider creating a security portal on your company intranet to provide ongoing resources and updates.

2. **Engagement and Evaluation:**
- o **Interactive Activities:** Include interactive activities such as attack simulations, security games and quizzes to make campaigns more engaging and educational. These activities help reinforce knowledge and practice of security best practices.
- o **Impact Assessment:** Measure the effectiveness of awareness campaigns through knowledge surveys, testing, and incident analysis to assess the impact on employee behavior. Use the results to adjust and improve future campaigns.

# Evaluate the Effectiveness of Training Programs Regularly

1. **Monitoring and Evaluation:**
- o **Knowledge Tests:** Conduct regular tests and assessments to measure employees' knowledge and understanding of the topics covered in training. Use quizzes, simulations and practical exercises to assess the application of knowledge.
- o **Feedback Surveys:** Conduct feedback surveys to collect information about employee perceptions of training

effectiveness. Ask about the clarity of the content, the applicability of the information and the level of satisfaction with the formats used.

2. **Adjustments and Improvements:**
   - **Results Analysis:** Analyze assessment and survey results to identify areas for improvement in training and awareness programs. Adjust content and methods based on identified needs and changes in the threat environment.
   - **Continuous Update:** Regularly update training materials and methods to reflect new threats and emerging best practices. Ensure training programs remain relevant and effective in addressing evolving security challenges.

## Conclusion

Ongoing training and awareness are critical components to effective information security strategies. By investing in developing robust programs and running effective awareness campaigns, organizations can strengthen their security posture, reduce the risk of incidents, and foster a culture of security among employees. Regularly evaluating and adjusting these programs will ensure they remain effective and relevant, contributing to a more robust defense against cyber threats.

# 6. Incident Response and Crisis Management

## Create and Maintain an Incident Response Plan

1. **Development of the Incident Response Plan:**
   o **Objective and Scope:** The incident response plan must clearly establish the objective of minimizing damage and restoring normal operations efficiently. Scope the plan to cover all types of incidents that could affect the organization, from cyberattacks to critical systems failures.
   o **Detailed Procedures:**
      ▪ **Identification:** Create a process for initial incident detection, which may include the use of event monitoring and analysis tools. Establish criteria to classify the severity of the incident and determine the need for an immediate response.
      ▪ **Containment:** Describe the actions necessary to limit the impact of the incident and prevent it from spreading. This may include disconnecting compromised systems, locking affected user accounts, or isolating network segments.
      ▪ **Eradication:** Define procedures to remove the root cause of the incident, which may involve eliminating malware, patching exploited vulnerabilities, or updating compromised systems.
      ▪ **Recovery:** Establish methods to restore systems and operations to their normal state. This includes recovering data from backups and validating the integrity of systems to ensure there are no remaining threats.
2. **Documentation and Communication:**
   o **Incident Log:** Keep detailed records of all incidents, including the timeline of events, actions taken and communication made. These records are essential for later analysis and to improve response to future incidents.

o **Review and Update:** Review the incident response plan regularly to reflect changes in the threat environment, the organization's infrastructure, and security best practices. Lessons learned from previous incidents should be incorporated to strengthen the plan.

# Establish and Train an Incident Response Team (CSIRT)

1. **Incident Response Team Training:**
o **Member Selection:** Build a dedicated incident response team (CSIRT) comprised of information security experts, systems administrators, and communications professionals. Each member must have complementary skills and knowledge to deal with various aspects of security incidents.
o **Roles and Responsibilities:** Clearly define the roles and responsibilities of each team member. Include roles such as incident coordinator, forensic analyst, crisis communicator, and technical support.
2. **Training and Simulations:**
o **Training Programs:** Develop ongoing training programs for staff, addressing both technical skills and crisis management competencies. Include topics such as forensic analysis techniques, effective communication, and stress management.
o **Simulations and Exercises:** Conduct regular incident simulations to test team readiness and response plan effectiveness. Use realistic scenarios to ensure that the team can apply the plan's procedures under pressure and time-limited conditions.

# Develop Communication Procedures for Crises and Data Leaks

1. **Communication Procedures During Crises:**
   - **Internal Communication:** Establish protocols to quickly inform leadership and affected departments about the crisis. Create a centralized communications channel to coordinate information dissemination and ensure a coordinated response.
   - **External Communication:** Develop procedures for communicating with customers, partners, and other external parties. Prepare public statements and specific communications for different stakeholders, ensuring clarity and transparency.
2. **Data Leak Notification Protocols:**
   - **Reporting to Regulators and Affected Parties:** Create procedures for reporting data breaches to regulators as required by regulations such as GDPR or CCPA. Develop notifications to inform affected individuals, detailing the nature of the breach, actions taken, and resources available for assistance.
   - **Transparency and Reputation Management:** Establish practices to manage the company's reputation during and after an incident. Ensure communication is transparent and actions taken are visible to build and maintain stakeholder trust.

# Review and Update Incident Response Plans After Events

1. **Post-Incident Analysis:**
   o    **Review and Assessment:** After an incident is resolved, conduct a detailed analysis to assess the effectiveness of the response and identify areas for improvement. Analyze response time, decisions made, and communication during the incident.
   o    **Lessons Learned:** Document lessons learned and strengths and weaknesses identified during the incident. Use this information to adjust and improve your incident response plan and associated procedures.
2. **Plan Update:**
   o    **Incorporation of Improvements:** Update the incident response plan based on lessons learned and changes in the threat environment and technology. Review and adjust procedures, team responsibilities, and communication protocols to ensure a more effective response to future incidents.
   o    **Regular Reassessment:** Conduct periodic reviews of the plan to ensure it remains relevant and effective. Incorporate new threats, technologies and best practices to keep the plan updated and aligned with the organization's needs.

# 7. Monitoring and Auditing

## Implement Continuous Monitoring of Systems and Networks

1. **Monitoring Tools and Technologies:**
   o    **Monitoring Solutions:** Use advanced monitoring tools to continuously monitor the security of systems

and networks. Tools like security information and event management (SIEM) systems can collect and correlate log data to identify patterns of suspicious behavior.

o **Log and Traffic Analysis:** Monitor event logs, network traffic, and user activity to detect anomalous activity. Set up alerts to notify your security team of potential incidents in real time.

2. **Response to Alerts and Incidents:**

o **Alert Analysis:** Develop procedures for analyzing and responding to alerts generated by monitoring tools. Assess the severity of alerts and determine appropriate actions, such as investigation or containment of potential incidents.

o **Incident Tracking:** Keep a record of all monitoring-related activities, including incident investigation and response. Use this information to improve the effectiveness of monitoring tools and processes.

# Conduct Regular Security and Compliance Audits

1. **Audit Planning and Execution:**

o **Audit Schedule:** Establish a schedule for regular security and compliance audits. Audits should cover all aspects of the organization's security practices, including policies, controls and processes.

o **Internal and External Auditors:** Consider using internal and external auditors to assess compliance with policies and regulations. External auditors can provide an unbiased perspective and identify areas for improvement that may not be evident to internal staff.

2. **Reports and Corrective Actions:**

o **Audit Reports:** Prepare detailed reports on

audit results, highlighting areas of compliance and non-compliance. Include recommendations to improve security and ensure compliance with policies and regulations.

o **Action Plans:** Develop action plans to address deficiencies identified during audits. Monitor the implementation of corrective actions and reassess the effectiveness of improvements made.

# Analyze and Report Security Metrics and Performance Indicators (KPIs)

1. **Definition of KPIs:**
o **Metrics Identification:** Select key performance indicators (KPIs) to measure the effectiveness of security initiatives. Examples of KPIs include the number of incidents detected, average response time, and the effectiveness of security controls.
o **Goal Setting:** Set specific goals for each KPI to evaluate the performance and progress of security initiatives.
2. **KPI Analysis and Reporting:**
o **Performance Assessment:** Review metrics and KPIs regularly to assess the effectiveness of security practices. Identify trends, patterns and areas that require attention or improvement.
o **Performance Reports:** Prepare detailed reports on security performance, highlighting KPI results and areas of success and improvement. Use these reports to inform leadership and support strategic decision-making in information security.

These sections provide a solid foundation for managing and responding to security incidents, ensuring that the organization is well prepared to deal with crises and maintains a proactive stance towards security and compliance.

# 8. Application and Systems Security

## Perform Penetration Testing and Security Assessments on Applications

1. **Conduct Regular Penetration Testing:**
   o **Purpose of Penetration Testing:** Carrying out penetration tests, also known as pen tests, is an essential practice for identifying and exploiting vulnerabilities in applications and systems. These tests simulate real attacks to assess the strength of defenses and identify weaknesses that could be exploited by malicious actors.
   o **Test Methodologies:**
      ▪ **Automated Tests:** They use automated tools to perform systematic scans and identify common vulnerabilities, such as SQL injections, cross-site scripting (XSS), and configuration flaws. These tests are effective in identifying known flaws and providing an overview of vulnerabilities.
      ▪ **Manual Tests:** They involve manual, in-depth analysis of applications to identify complex vulnerabilities that may not be detected by automated tools. Experienced testers simulate sophisticated attack techniques, exploiting logic flaws and application-specific vulnerabilities.
   o **Testing Process:**
      ▪ **Planning and Scope:** Define the scope of testing, including systems, applications and components to be evaluated. Establish clear goals and expectations with stakeholders.

- **Execution and Reporting:** Conduct testing according to plan, documenting all findings in detail. Create a comprehensive report that describes the vulnerabilities found, their potential impact, and recommendations for mitigation.
- **Remediation and Reassessment:** Work with responsible teams to fix identified vulnerabilities and perform additional testing to validate the effectiveness of the fixes.

2. **Use Security Assessments:**
   - **Objective of Assessments:** Security assessments are intended to examine the effectiveness of existing protection measures and the overall security robustness of applications and systems. They complement penetration testing by providing a detailed view of application security.
   - **Types of Assessments:**
     - **Source Code Reviews:** They review the source code of applications to identify vulnerabilities such as coding flaws and exposure of sensitive data. Static code analysis tools (SAST) can help detect security issues during development.
     - **Architecture and Design Reviews:** They evaluate application architecture and design to ensure that security controls are properly implemented at all layers. Check segregation of duties, access controls and protection of sensitive data.

# Implement Secure Development Practices (DevSecOps)

1. **Integrate Security into the Development Lifecycle:**
   - **DevSecOps Objective:** DevSecOps is an approach that

aims to integrate security practices into the software development lifecycle from the beginning. Rather than treating security as a final step, DevSecOps promotes the continuous incorporation of security measures throughout the development process.

- **Practices and Tools:**
  - **Security in the Planning Phase:** Incorporate security requirements into project specifications and planning. Perform risk analyzes and define mitigation strategies to identify and address potential vulnerabilities early.
  - **Security During Development:** Utilize static (SAST) and dynamic (DAST) code analysis tools to identify and fix vulnerabilities during development. Integrate security checks into your CI/CD pipeline to perform automated testing for each integration.
  - **Automation and Integration:** Automate security testing, validations, and code reviews to ensure security practices are continuously and consistently applied. Use CI/CD pipelines to incorporate security into each phase of development.

2. **Promote Safety Culture:**
  - **Training and Awareness:** Provide ongoing training on secure development practices for developers and other stakeholders. Promote a security culture that emphasizes the importance of identifying and fixing vulnerabilities during development.
  - **Feedback and Continuous Improvement:** Establish feedback channels on security practices and respond to discovered vulnerabilities. Use lessons learned to improve security processes and practices and to better respond to future challenges.

# Manage and Protect the Lifecycle of Applications and Systems

1. **Security During Development:**
   o **Definition of Security Requirements:** Establish security requirements from the design and planning phase. Make sure practices like encryption, strong authentication, and access control are incorporated from the beginning of development.
   o **Review and Validation:** Conduct regular security reviews during development to ensure that security requirements are met and that the application is protected against known threats.
2. **Security in Implementation and Maintenance:**
   o **Configuration Management:** Use configuration management tools to monitor and apply secure configurations to systems and applications. Ensure that settings comply with security policies and are adjusted as needed.
   o **Updates and Patches:** Keep all systems and applications updated with the latest security patches to fix known vulnerabilities and protect against new threats. Establish an efficient patch management process to ensure timely application of updates.
3. **Secure Decommissioning of Obsolete Systems:**
   o **Deactivation and Removal:** Develop procedures to safely decommission and remove obsolete systems. Ensure that all data is correctly removed and sensitive information is destroyed to prevent data leaks.
   o **Documentation and Auditing:** Document the decommissioning process and perform audits to ensure security measures were applied appropriately. Maintain detailed records for future reference and compliance

audits.

These practices are crucial to ensuring the security of applications and systems throughout their lifecycle, from initial development to maintenance and eventual decommissioning. Effectively implementing these practices helps protect against vulnerabilities and threats, ensuring the integrity and confidentiality of the organization's data and systems.

# 9. Security in Cloud and Hybrid Environments

## Implement Specific Security Controls for Cloud Environments

1. **Data Encryption:**
   o **Encryption in Transit and at Rest:** Ensure data is encrypted both in transit and at rest. Utilize strong encryption protocols such as TLS (Transport Layer Security) to protect data in transit and advanced encryption algorithms such as AES (Advanced Encryption Standard) for data at rest.
   o **Key Management:** Implement secure practices for managing cryptographic keys, including regularly rotating and securing keys in hardware security modules (HSM) whenever possible.
2. **Identity and Access Management (IAM):**
   o **Granular Access Policies:** Define and implement granular access policies that ensure only authorized users can access specific resources. Use features like groups and roles to apply permissions efficiently.
   o **Multi-Factor Authentication (MFA):** Require MFA for all administrator accounts and for users accessing

sensitive data. This adds an additional layer of security beyond traditional passwords.

3. **Network Security:**
   o        **Virtual Perimeter Security:** Use virtual firewalls and virtual private networks (VPNs) to secure communication between your cloud instances and your company's internal network.
   o        **Network Segmentation:** Implement network segmentation to isolate different types of traffic and protect critical resources from potential attacks.

4. **Security Policies and Settings:**
   o   **Secure Settings:** Apply security settings recommended by cloud providers and industry best practices. Continuously monitor configurations to ensure they comply with security policies.
   o        **Regular Security Assessments:** Perform regular security assessments to identify and remediate potential vulnerabilities in security configuration and policies.

# Ensuring Data Protection in Hybrid and Multi-Cloud Environments

1. **Uniform Security Policies:**
   o   **Policy Integration:** Develop and implement security policies that are consistent across hybrid and multi-cloud environments. This includes uniform application of access controls, encryption and monitoring.
   o        **Centralized Management:** Utilize centralized management tools to enforce and monitor security policies across different platforms and cloud providers.

2. **Integrated Security Tools:**
   o        **Multi-Cloud Security Solutions:** Adopt security

solutions that provide comprehensive visibility and control across multi-cloud environments. Tools like endpoint security solutions and security information and event management (SIEM) platforms can help monitor and secure all of your cloud instances.

o **Automation and Orchestration:** Use automation and orchestration to ensure consistent application of security policies and to quickly respond to incidents across different environments.

3. **Monitoring and Response:**

o **Continuous Monitoring:** Implement monitoring tools that provide real-time visibility into the security of your cloud instances. Monitor event logs, network traffic, and user activity to detect and respond to potential threats.

o **Incident Response:** Develop procedures to respond to security incidents that may affect multiple cloud platforms. Establish communication and coordination protocols to effectively manage and mitigate the impacts of incidents.

# Monitor and Manage Access and Security on Cloud Platforms

1. **Specific Monitoring Tools:**

o **Cloud Native Security Solutions:** Use tools provided by cloud providers to monitor the security of your instances. Many platforms offer built-in features for activity monitoring and threat detection.

o **Third Party Tools:** Consider using third-party security tools that offer advanced monitoring and analysis capabilities for cloud environments.

2. **Access Control and Authentication:**

- o    **Access Control Policies:** Establish and enforce strict access control policies to ensure that only authorized users can access cloud resources. Use attribute- and role-based policies to manage permissions at a granular level.
- o    **Multi-Factor Authentication:** Apply MFA to all accounts that have access to critical resources. This helps protect against unauthorized access, even if credentials are compromised.

3. **Audit and Compliance:**

- o    **Continuous Audit:** Perform ongoing audits to verify compliance with security policies and regulations. Use auditing tools to generate reports and identify areas that need improvement.
- o    **Reports and Records:** Maintain detailed records of all access activities and security events. These records are essential for incident investigation and meeting regulatory requirements.

Security in cloud and hybrid environments requires a comprehensive approach that integrates specific controls to protect data and resources, applies uniform security policies, and uses advanced tools for monitoring and management. Effectively implementing these practices helps protect the integrity, confidentiality, and availability of data and systems in a dynamic, multifaceted cloud landscape.

# 10. Innovation and the Future of Security

## Monitor and Adopt Safe Technological Innovations

1. **Monitoring Technological Trends:**
   o **Research and Analysis:** Stay up to date with the latest technological innovations and their security implications. This includes following research publications, security expert blogs, and industry trend reports.
   o **Participation in Events:** Attend conferences, seminars and webinars about new technologies and security. These events provide insights into emerging innovations and best practices for implementing them safely.

2. **Assessment of New Technologies:**
   o **Risk Analysis:** Before adopting new technologies, conduct a risk analysis to identify potential vulnerabilities and security impacts. Consider conducting security testing and impact assessments.
   o **Compliance and Regulations:** Verify that new technology complies with applicable security and privacy regulations. Assess how the technology aligns with the organization's security policies and requirements.

3. **Training and Qualification:**
   o **Continuous Training:** Invest in training and qualifications for the security team on new technologies and their implications. This ensures the team is equipped to manage and protect against threats associated with technological innovations.
   o **Certifications and Courses:** Encourage staff to obtain certifications in new areas of technology and security to enhance their skills and knowledge.

# Assess and Prepare for New

# Security Threats and Trends

1. **Emerging Threat Analysis:**
   o **Research and Intelligence:** Utilize threat intelligence tools and services to monitor and identify new attack techniques and emerging trends. This includes malware analysis, social engineering techniques, and zero-day attacks.
   o **Simulations and Scenarios:** Conduct simulations and attack exercises to test your organization's preparedness against new threats. This helps identify gaps and improve incident response.
2. **Update Response Plans:**
   o **Regular Review:** Regularly review and update incident response plans and mitigation strategies to incorporate new threats and attack techniques. Updates should reflect lessons learned from previous incidents and new threat information.
   o **Adaptation of Policies:** Adjust policies and procedures to address new threats and ensure existing controls are effective against emerging attack techniques.
3. **Collaboration and Information Sharing:**
   o **Participation in Communities:** Get involved in security communities and working groups to share information about new threats and best practices. Collaboration with other organizations can provide valuable insights and improve resilience against threats.
   o **Partnerships with Suppliers:** Work with security vendors to obtain updates and patches related to new vulnerabilities and threats. Maintain an open dialogue to ensure you are informed about the latest security threats and solutions.

# Invest in Emerging Technologies to Strengthen Security Posture

1. **Artificial Intelligence and Machine Learning:**
   - **Detection and Response:** Invest in solutions based on artificial intelligence (AI) and machine learning to improve threat detection and incident response. These technologies can identify anomalous patterns and suspicious behaviors with greater accuracy.
   - **Security Automation:** Use AI to automate security tasks such as log analysis, incident response, and vulnerability management, enabling a faster, more efficient response.
2. **Blockchain and Data Security:**
   - **Data Integrity:** Explore the use of blockchain to ensure data integrity and transparency. Blockchain can be used to create immutable and auditable records, providing an additional layer of security against fraud and data manipulation.
   - **Authentication and Identity:** Evaluate the use of blockchain to improve authentication security and identity management, offering a decentralized and attack-resistant approach.
3. **Advanced Security Technologies:**
   - **Cloud and Container Security:** Consider advanced technologies to secure cloud and container environments, such as micro-segmentation, container security policy management, and cloud-native security solutions.
   - **Privacy Solutions:** Invest in technologies that protect data privacy, such as anonymization solutions and advanced encryption techniques to protect sensitive information.

4. **Assessment and Implementation:**

   o **Proofs of Concept:** Conduct proofs of concept (PoC) to evaluate the feasibility and effectiveness of emerging technologies before full implementation. Test solutions in controlled environments to ensure they meet your organization's security needs.

   o **ROI and Cost-Benefit:** Evaluate the return on investment (ROI) and cost-effectiveness of emerging technologies to ensure the investment brings tangible improvements to your security posture.

Continuous innovation is essential to keep information security up to date and effective. By tracking and adopting new technologies, assessing new threats, and investing in emerging technologies, an organization can strengthen its security posture and be better prepared to face future cybersecurity challenges.

**Conclusion**

The career in information security is one of the most promising and challenging today. Professionals who are dedicated to constant improvement are rewarded with excellent job opportunities and attractive salaries.

Throughout this book, I have presented the main concepts and practices of information security, from the fundamentals to the most advanced topics. I hope the content has been useful to you and that it contributes to your professional growth.

I thank all the readers who followed this book until the end. If you liked the content, please leave a review on Amazon and share your impressions with me on social media. Search for "Igor Doin" and give me feedback on your reading, this is the most important thing for me: knowing that I helped you with something on your journey :)

Thank you and see you next time reading!